THE ZULU PRINCIPLE

MAKING EXTRAORDINARY PROFITS
FROM ORDINARY SHARES

WARNING

Stockmarket investments, and income, can go down as well as up. They may also have poor marketability. When you seek advice, also ask about marketability. The shares referred to in the text of this book are for illustrative purposes only and are not an invitation to deal in them. The book was completed in June 1992 and since then market conditions have changed. Neither the publishers nor the author accept any legal responsibility for the contents of the work, which is not a substitute for detailed professional advice. Readers should conduct their investment activity through an appropriately authorized person.

THE ZULU PRINCIPLE

MAKING EXTRAORDINARY PROFITS
FROM ORDINARY SHARES

JIM SLATER

ORION

To Helen, my best investment

First published in Great Britain in 1992 by
Orion
An imprint of Orion Books Ltd.
Orion House, 5 Upper St. Martin's Lane, London WC2H 9EA
Reprinted November 1992
Reprinted December 1992

A CIP catalogue record for this book is available
from the British Library

ISBN 1 85797 095 0

Design and production: Tim Plummer, Peter Higgins
Cover Design: Orion

Printed in Great Britain by
Butler & Tanner Ltd., Frome, Somerset

CONTENTS

ACKNOWLEDGEMENTS

I would like to thank Jeremy Utton for the idea that I should write a book on investment. His suggestion coincided with my son, Mark, finding a dearth of British books on the subject.

I would also like to thank Jeremy and my friends Sir James Goldsmith, Ian Watson, Bryan Quinton, George Finlay, Ralph Baber and Peter Greaves for reading the proofs and making some very constructive and helpful suggestions for improving the text.

Thanks are also due to Dr. Marc Faber for allowing me to quote him so extensively on Emerging Markets. Also a special word of appreciation to Warren Buffett for writing and saying so many interesting things about investment and allowing me to use them in this book.

I am also grateful to Brian Marber for the interview on technical analysis, for his comments and for his amusing stories.

My two sons have also been most helpful: Christopher by drawing his two cartoons and the bull and the bear, and Mark for long days of diligent work on the proofs, for his time and effort on research and for his many ideas for uplifting the content.

I would not live to tell the tale unless I included Pam Hall, my long-suffering secretary, who has typed most chapters so many times that she knows some of them by heart.

PREFACE

ONE OF MY SONS IS INTERESTED IN THE STOCKMARKET. After reading a number of quite advanced American books on investment, he asked me if I could recommend a British book of a similar nature. I searched my mind and then the book shops, only to find that there was nothing beyond the primer stage. Market forces usually begin to fill a gap; hence my decision to write this book. I have no doubt that many others will follow.

My intention is to show you how to become a very successful investor. My problem is that I do not know if you are an aspiring trainee stockbroker; an accountant or a lawyer who has an understanding of many of the rudiments of investment; or someone who is in a very different line of business or who has retired after a life-time in industry. I do not want to bore the people who understand the basics, so I shall assume that you are connected with the business of investment in some way or that you have read the Glossary at the end of this book. Either way, you will then know the difference between an ordinary share, a preference share and a convertible debenture; the meaning of terms like price earnings ratio, dividend yield and asset value; and the effect and significance of scrip and rights issues.

There are a number of different methods and areas of investment, some of which I will explain to you in much more detail in later chapters:

SMALL DYNAMIC GROWTH COMPANIES

Fast-growing companies with market capitalisations ranging from £5m to £100m are not researched frequently by the investment community, so their shares are often exceptionally attractive.

TURNAROUND SITUATIONS AND CYCLICALS

Companies that have been hit hard by a recessionary environment or other exceptional factors are often due for a rebound. These situations involve cyclical companies and those which have recently had a change of management.

SHELLS

Shells are another exciting medium of investment. These are often very small companies that have a quotation, a small, nondescript business of little account and occasionally some cash. Usually, the idea of the incoming entrepreneur is to obtain a back-door quotation for his company, which has too short a record, or some other shortcoming which precludes a more conventional route. There are many examples of successful and sometimes infamous shells from Hanson and Williams Holdings to Polly Peck and Parkfield. The ride can be very exciting.

ASSET SITUATIONS

Some of my friends invest solely in companies in which the shares have a market value less than the worth of the underlying businesses on a break-up. These value investors wait for a trigger, such as a bid or the arrival of new management, to revitalise the assets and bring them up to their full earnings potential. The shares then begin to appreciate in value.

LEADING STOCKS

Companies in the FT-SE 100 Index usually offer the comfort of size and rarely fail completely. These kinds of shares can also be sold much more easily even in bad markets. They are, however, well analysed by the investment community, increasing the difficulty of finding a real bargain. I intend to give you some selective criteria that should improve your investment performance with leading shares in this country. I have also found that my criteria work extremely well in America and most overseas markets.

If you need to read the Glossary please do so now, as I am anxious to show you how to make some money by using an approach that I have named 'The Zulu Principle'. You will not be spending any time on gilts, preference shares, loan stocks and the Japanese market. Instead, you will concentrate upon five different ways of making money by investing in ordinary shares before you finally select one method or perhaps two that suit your temperament.

I first named this approach 'The Zulu Principle' after my wife read a four page article on Zulus in *Reader's Digest*. From that moment onwards she knew more than me about Zulus. If she had then borrowed all the available books on the subject from the local library and read them carefully she would have known more about Zulus than most people in Surrey. If she had decided subsequently to visit South Africa, live for six months in a Zulu kraal and study all the available literature on Zulus at a South African University, she would have become one of the leading authorities in Great Britain and possibly the world. The key point is that the history of Zulus and their habits and customs today is a clearly defined and narrow area of knowledge into which my wife would have invested a disproportionate amount of her time and effort, with the result that she would have become an acknowledged expert. The study of this noble people might not have been profitable, but there are many other very specialised subjects that would have been very rewarding financially.

ZULU WARRIOR

I now intend to show you how to use The Zulu Principle with your investments. You will achieve your objective, like Montgomery and Napoleon before him, by concentrating your attack.

1

WINNING

INVESTMENT IS NO DIFFERENT FROM ANY OTHER GAME. Winning is much more fun than losing, and luck and skill both play their part. Bad players often complain about their luck, but as Gary Player, the famous golfer, said, 'The harder you work, the luckier you get.' Elmer Letterman put this another way, 'Luck is when preparation meets opportunity.' Let me show you how to prepare for investment and become a winner.

There is a great deal of luck in Monopoly. If you have bad dice, you might travel around the board paying huge amounts of tax and end up sitting in jail while your opponent snatches all the good sites. However, there is a small skill element in the game, and over a long period better players will win more often. Let us analyse the skill. The light blue properties — Pentonville Road, Euston Road and The Angel Islington — give the highest rental return of 159% compared with only 101% from the worst. The orange sites — Vine Street, Marlborough Street and Bow Street — are next best with a return of 141%. This yield is calculated by taking the total cost of buying all three orange sites and building hotels, which in this case is £2060, and comparing this figure with the rental on the three hotels, which would be a total of £2900. At first blush the light blue sites would seem to be better than the orange ones, but Vine Street, Marlborough Street and Bow Street are my favourites because of another important factor — the frequency with which your opponents are likely to land upon them. Firstly, there is a card in Chance 'Go back three spaces', and from one position this would put them on Vine Street. Secondly, the orange sites are a dice throw away from jail, which means that other players being released are more likely to land upon them. Thirdly, there are two other cards in Chance, one of which directs a player to 'Take a trip to Marylebone Station' and the other to 'Advance to Pall Mall'. Following these directions bypasses the light blue sites completely and leaves your opponents poised to visit the orange sites.

A further Monopoly guideline is to build quickly once you have a complete site, even at the expense of mortgaging other incomplete sites to do so. For example, the loss of rent on the Strand would be only £18 but £100 out of the mortgage proceeds of £110 could be used to buy an extra house on Bow Street. The first house takes the rent from £14 to £70 to give a gain of £56, and the difference rises to as much as £350 when the third house is added. Subject therefore to keeping a prudent cash reserve, you should mortgage all incomplete sites and use the proceeds to build rapidly.

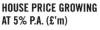

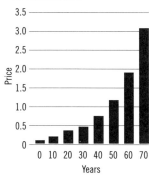

Before you participate in the game of investment, you should make sure that you acquire the necessary skill and that you can afford the stakes. I strongly recommend that you first invest in your own house or flat. In June 1992, property is in the doldrums, but for that reason it is a far better buy than a few years ago at the height of the property boom. As a long-term investment you can hardly do better, and there is a big bonus — you live in your house with enjoyment. Even with inflation at 5% per annum, a house costing £100,000 would tend to keep in line and, in a man's normal life-span, appreciate in value over the seventy years to more than £3,000,000. The arithmetic is even better than this though, because most people would have an affordable mortgage, so the return on their net outlay would be much enhanced. In addition, there is still no capital gains tax on owner-occupied houses, and there is some tax relief on mortgage interest. You cannot afford to invest in the stockmarket before taking advantage of these privileges.

You also need to ensure that you have some money set aside for school fees, illness and a rainy day. The money that you are going to use for investment in shares has to be *patient* money that will not need to be withdrawn suddenly.

In the investment game your main problem is that you will be up against full time professionals who eat, drink and sleep investment. They have readier access to the companies in which they are likely to invest, more general information at their disposal and they are regularly bombarded with brokers' circulars and investment recommendations. In addition, brokers hoping for more business give the institutions their best possible service and keenest terms.

So you start off at a considerable disadvantage. There is a way to win, but unless you are prepared to dedicate a few hours a week to your investments, you will have no hope of succeeding. I suggest an average of at least half an hour a day — thirty minutes that I hope you will look forward to and enjoy.

To compete you need to develop an edge, so let me encourage you now with a few ideas. First you must find a market niche that is under-exploited by the professionals. Most leading brokers, professional investors and institutions concentrate their analytical skills on major companies with market capitalisations of £500m or more. The reasons for this are obvious. If a broker can produce a good argument for buying or selling a leading stock, institutions will be able to deal in volume, and a large turnover (with hefty commissions for the broker) will be the likely result. The institutions prefer leading stocks because their marketability is better. When they come to take a profit or cut a loss, they can usually deal in volume at a very keen price.

Investment is essentially the arbitrage of ignorance. The successful investor believes he knows something that other investors do not fully appreciate. There is very little that is unknown about leading stocks, so in that area of the market there is hardly any ignorance to arbitrage. GEC, Glaxo and ICI are the subject of hundreds of brokers' circulars every year. In contrast, some smaller stocks are not written up at all and others by only one or two brokers. Most leading brokers cannot spare the time and money to research smaller stocks. You are therefore more likely to find a bargain (with some ignorance to arbitrage) in this relatively under-exploited area of the stockmarket. This is a possible niche for you.

The second factor that gives you an advantage over professionals is that they usually have to invest a massive amount of money. Many of them manage billions. Try to imagine some of the problems you would have looking after just a paltry £500m:

1. You would find it difficult to invest meaningfully in stocks with smaller market capitalisations. You will see in later chapters that this would be a big handicap.

2. You would have to spread your investments over at least 200 stocks and probably many more. By the time you came to your 100th selection it would be obviously less attractive than your 50th, considerably less attractive than your 10th, and infinitely less attractive than your first choice. Contrast this with managing a small portfolio in which you can concentrate upon an average of ten prime selections. A tremendous advantage!

3. As the manager of an institutional portfolio with 200 stocks or more under your control, the incidence of your own input from personal knowledge would be far less. You would be closeted in the Square Mile for most of your working day instead of being out and about with your eyes and ears open. As a private investor you have the advantage — you might notice that Sainsbury is opening several new supermarkets or that Alexon shops are especially crowded. You might hear that a local quoted engineering company is taking on another 100 people or that a friend is delighted with his new computer. Once you begin to think in terms of your investment portfolio, any information of this nature can be an important lead. The advantage of this kind of personal awareness has to be spread very thinly across an institutional portfolio, whereas in yours it will have a major impact.

A further aid to overcoming expert competition is to apply The Zulu Principle to investment within your chosen niche market. I will show you five different approaches and suggest that you specialise in one of them. To begin with, we will look at a method of investing in relatively small companies that have shown strong past earnings growth, have future potential and appear to be rated inadequately by the market. I have profited most from investing in this kind of share and for that reason will deal with this system in considerable detail. The first ten chapters should help you to get the feel of the investment business before you progress to separate chapters on turnarounds, shells and asset situations. You should then be able to judge which approach will best suit your temperament. You need patience for asset situations and smaller growth stocks, in contrast to the more immediate pain or pleasure that will be felt by investing in shells and turnarounds. Investment in overseas markets and leading UK stocks are the subjects of separate chapters in which I set out some selective criteria for improving portfolio performance.

Let us now look at smaller growth stocks in more detail. You are searching for those that appear to be inadequately rated by the market. Sometimes there is a good reason for the market's lack of enthusiasm. Your skill element will be finding out which companies deserve a much higher rating and which do not. Needless to say, you cannot expect to be right all of the time, but when you make a really good choice, your capital profit will surprise you and far outweigh the losses from occasional mistakes.

There are two basic reasons for growth shares increasing in price and providing you with substantial capital profits in the process. The first is the earnings growth itself. If a share is priced at ten times earnings and in the next set of results shows 25% earnings growth, all things being equal the shares will naturally appreciate by about 25%. The second reason for an uplift in price then comes into play. During the few months following the results, the market would be very likely to re-rate the shares to a more appropriate multiple which for a company growing at 25% p.a. would be at least 20 and probably much higher. The status change in the multiple would increase your gain from 25% to 150%.

$$100 \; + \; 25 \quad \text{x} \quad \frac{20}{10} \; = \; 250$$

$$\text{Less original investment} \qquad 100$$

$$\text{GAIN} \qquad 150$$

Another factor that contributes to the success of investment in smaller companies is that generally speaking elephants don't gallop. The last year or so has been exceptional, and a few elephants have charged both here and in America, whereas smaller companies have lagged behind. The Hoare Govett Small Companies Index beat the FT All-Share Index in 27 of the last 37 years. Over the last ten years, the HGSC Index under-performed the market by 6%. 1989, 1990 and 1991 were all poor years for small companies, with three successive years of under-performance occurring for the first time. This reflects the increasing dominance of institutions in the UK market and their preference for leading stocks. There is also no doubt that in recessionary times smaller companies have a higher operational risk. Nevertheless, I believe that the potential rewards more than counterbalance this, making carefully selected, small to medium-sized companies an even better buy today.

Sainsbury, one of our most successful companies, is at the time of writing valued by the stockmarket at about £8bn. The management will find this vast capitalisation very hard to double during the next year or so. The rating is already high at 18 times historic earnings, and most institutions have their quota of Sainsbury shares. Smaller companies have more to gain from new investors discovering them, and as their following develops, so does the share price. For example, the shares of a little company like The MTL Instruments Group (which you will hear more about later) had no difficulty in doubling in twelve months. In February 1991, the shares were 124p, with the company on a multiple of 11 times earnings capitalising at £21.7m. One year later the shares were 275p. 1990 earnings were 20% up on the previous year, and 1991 earnings looked like increasing by a similar amount. The historic price earnings ratio was re-rated from 11 to 16, and hey presto by February 1992 the market capitalisation had increased from £21.7m to over £48m.

BEFORE WE SETTLE DOWN TO WORK, LET ME RECAP MY RECOMMENDATIONS TO YOU:

1. Make a conscious decision to devote at least three hours a week to your investments.

2. Read the whole of this book before selecting an approach to investment that you feel would be most suitable for your temperament.

3. When you have selected your niche market become as expert as possible in that particular area of investment. As Warren Buffett, the legendary American investor, says, it is not necessary for an investor to know more than one thing, but he certainly has to know that.

We will now move on to look in much greater detail at my system for investing in the dynamic growth of smaller companies.

2

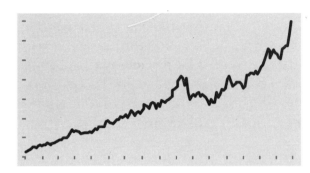

SMALL DYNAMIC GROWTH SHARES

IN 1959, I WAS COMMERCIAL DIRECTOR OF AEC LIMITED, TRAVELLING EXTENSIVELY OVERSEAS. On a visit to Spain I contracted a viral illness, the after-effects of which lasted for several years. I began to worry that I might not be able to carry on with such a strenuous job for any length of time. I decided that there was only one answer — I had to build some capital and an alternative source of income.

It was no accident that I chose Stock Exchange investment. Shares could be a profitable hobby easily managed while I still retained my job. The only problem was how to become relatively expert in the chosen specialist subject.

At the time there were two weekly investment magazines, *The Stock Exchange Gazette* and the *Investors Chronicle*, now both merged under one title. I decided to apply the approach that I subsequently named 'The Zulu Principle'. To begin with I purchased two years' back copies of both magazines, and during a convalescent period in Bournemouth read through them page by page. I was convinced that the stockmarket winners of the past would have some common characteristics. If, with the benefit of hindsight, I could develop a formula based upon these characteristics, I was sure that I would be able to make my fortune.

I soon discovered that shares with a rising trend in earnings that also seemed to be on a relatively inexpensive multiple (earnings yield at the time) out-performed the rest of the market by a wide margin. A few failed to do so, and this made it essential to find out why and to devise some additional criteria that would help to erect a safety net under my selections.

During the following year I honed my system before putting it into practice — with astounding success. The market was in a bullish phase, which was obviously a helpful factor. As I began to succeed I gave investment advice to a number of friends, and also formed a small investment club for the executives of Leyland and AEC. I also gave investment advice to my boss, Donald Stokes, and a number of other colleagues. Like a child with a new toy, I wrote to Nigel Lawson, who was at the time the City Editor of the *Sunday Telegraph*. He thought my ideas had merit, and asked me to write a column each month under the pseudonym of 'Capitalist'.

Nigel Lawson introduced the first article with these words:

'Today we welcome a new contributor to the City Pages of the *Sunday Telegraph* — 'Capitalist'. This is the pseudonym of a director of a number of well-known industrial companies in Britain and overseas who, in his spare time, has developed a highly successful new approach to investment. In this first article he explains his methods and selects the first three shares for his portfolio. In subsequent articles he will add further shares to the portfolio and review its progress to date.'

I explained in the article that I was looking for shares with an above-average earnings yield (the equivalent today would be a below-average price earnings ratio) coupled with above average growth prospects, and I outlined nine important investment criteria. It is interesting to look back on them, and I quote directly from the article:

'1. The dividend yield must be at least 4 per cent.
 2. Equity earnings must have increased in at least four out of the last five years.
 3. Equity earnings must have at least doubled over the last four years.
 4. The latest Chairman's statement must be optimistic.
 5. The company must be in a reasonably liquid position.

6. The company must not be vulnerable to exceptional factors.
7. The shares must have a reasonable asset value.
8. The company should not be family controlled.
9. The shares should have votes.'

The system worked — the Capitalist portfolio appreciated in value by 68.9% against the market average of only 3.6% during the same two year period from 1963 to 1965.

Since then market conditions have changed, and I have had a further twenty-seven years' investment experience. Needless to say I have modified, improved and added to my original criteria. Let me set them out for you as they are today, broadly in order of importance, together with a few explanatory notes which will be elaborated upon in later chapters:

1

A POSITIVE GROWTH RATE IN EARNINGS PER SHARE IN AT LEAST FOUR OF THE LAST FIVE YEARS

This one is unchanged. The odd hiccup must be allowed for, but otherwise look for steady growth of at least 15% per annum. The word 'steady' eliminates cyclical stocks.

A shorter record can be acceptable if there has been a recent sharp acceleration in earnings growth which might be due to new factors, which would make the historic earnings less relevant.

2

A LOW PRICE EARNINGS RATIO RELATIVE TO THE GROWTH RATE

Do not pay an excessive price for the future earnings you are buying. Look for a modest P/E ratio in relation to the earnings growth. There is an easy way of measuring the value you get for your money which is explained in the next chapter.

3

THE CHAIRMAN'S STATEMENT MUST BE OPTIMISTIC

If the chairman is pessimistic, earnings growth could be at an end. Watch with bated breath for his statement and for the interim results.

4
STRONG LIQUIDITY, LOW BORROWINGS AND HIGH CASH FLOW

Look for self-financing companies that generate cash. Avoid companies that are capital intensive and are always requiring more money for new machinery or even worse, for the replacement of old machinery at a vastly higher cost. Of course, capital expenditure is essential, but some companies simply eat cash, whereas others spit it out.

There are two ways of checking liquidity. The first is very simple — see if the company usually has a positive cash balance. Watch out for overdrafts and short-term loans on the other side of the balance sheet. You are looking for net cash. The second method is to determine the cash flow by analysing the accounts. You will learn how to do this. Meanwhile simply remember that you are trying to find companies that generate cash.

5
COMPETITIVE ADVANTAGE

The ideal business is one you can rely upon to produce increased earnings per share year after year. This reliability is usually based on the competitive advantage of well-known brand names, patents, copyrights, market dominance or a strong position in a niche business.

Coca Cola and Guinness are examples of businesses with strong brand names and market dominance. MTL Instruments is an example of a leading company in the niche business of intrinsic safety, including anti-explosive devices. An oil company buying a safety device that would help to prevent its oil rig from blowing up would not quibble too much about the price. Photo-Me International and Rentokil are other examples of companies with strong names and distinct niches.

PHOTO-ME BOOTH

You are trying to identify businesses which are not operating in an over-crowded market where intense competition will erode margins. The key points are that the product or service the company is supplying should not be easy to substitute; and new entries into the industry should be hard to envisage. A quick way of obtaining an idea of a company's relative strength in its industry is to examine pre-tax profit margins and the return on capital employed.

6
SOMETHING NEW

....

You want shares to have a story. Something new. Something that has happened relatively recently: a new factor in the industry like the failure of Harry Goodman's International Leisure Group in the holiday business, with Owners Abroad and Airtours benefiting massively from the removal of major competition; a new palm-top computer from Psion that swept the board at an American computer show. A new Chief Executive from a very successful firm like Glaxo or Hanson is one of the most reliable new factors because the benefits will be far-reaching and on-going. Greg Hutchings from Hanson joining F.H.Tomkins is an obvious and very successful example. All of these new factors are potential reasons for a substantial increase in future earnings and form the basis of the story upon which the shares will be bought.

AIRTOURS BROCHURES

7
A SMALL MARKET CAPITALISATION

....

As elephants don't gallop, you should give preference to companies with a small market capitalisation in the region of £10m-£50m, with an outside limit, in most cases, of £100m.

8
HIGH RELATIVE STRENGTH OF THE SHARES COMPARED
WITH THE MARKET

....

Sometimes shares perform poorly in the market in spite of very appealing fundamentals. Other investors may be selling after becoming aware of problems that you have not yet identified. Your broker should be able to let you have copies of Datastream charts (like the one overleaf) showing the relative performance of your chosen shares against the market. If the shares are not keeping up with the market, you should be on red alert. At the time of purchase, as a quick rule-of-thumb cross-check, make sure that the *growth* shares you select are within 15% of their maximum prices during the previous two years.

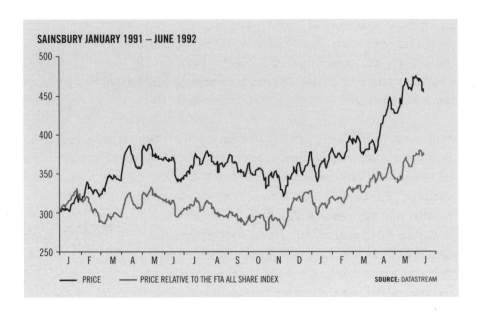

SAINSBURY JANUARY 1991 – JUNE 1992

— PRICE   — PRICE RELATIVE TO THE FTA ALL SHARE INDEX   **SOURCE:** DATASTREAM

9
A DIVIDEND YIELD

The dividend yield can be well below my original 4%, provided that dividends paid are growing in line with earnings. Some institutions or funds will not invest in the shares of companies which do not pay dividends. We are anxious not to preclude any of them from participating in our selections.

10
A REASONABLE ASSET POSITION

Very few UK growth shares in a dynamic phase are priced near to or below book value. Although you should welcome the comfort of a strong asset position, remember that book values are often unreliable. A property value could easily be overstated, whereas an excellent brand name may be in the books for next to nothing.

11
MANAGEMENT SHOULD HAVE A SIGNIFICANT SHAREHOLDING

You want the Directors to have a significant shareholding in relation to their personal finances — the actual amount of money involved is relatively unimportant. You are looking for shareholder-orientated management that will look after your interests with the 'owner's eye'. Avoid companies which still have two classes of shares, one of which gives extra votes to management. The ideal scenario is for management to have about 20% of the company so they are highly motivated but cannot block a bid.

There is no doubt that out of all of the above factors, the one that matters most is the relative cheapness of the P/E ratio in comparison with the growth rate. As you will see in later chapters many of the other criteria help to form a protective safety net around this fundamental requirement.

Before we progress any further let me whet your appetite with an example of a share that fulfilled my criteria in early 1991. As mentioned earlier, MTL Instruments is in the growing business of making safety devices for oil rigs, boiler rooms and chemical plants. Let us check off the statistics as they were in March 1991:

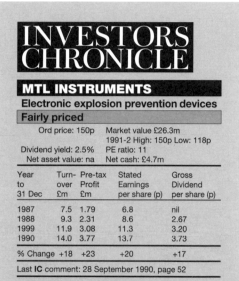

INVESTORS CHRONICLE

MTL INSTRUMENTS
Electronic explosion prevention devices
Fairly priced

Ord price: 150p   Market value £26.3m
                  1991-2 High: 150p Low: 118p
Dividend yield: 2.5%   PE ratio: 11
Net asset value: na   Net cash: £4.7m

Year to 31 Dec	Turnover £m	Pre-tax Profit £m	Stated Earnings per share (p)	Gross Dividend per share (p)
1987	7.5	1.79	6.8	nil
1988	9.3	2.31	8.6	2.67
1999	11.9	3.08	11.3	3.20
1990	14.0	3.77	13.7	3.73
% Change	+18	+23	+20	+17

Last **IC** comment: 28 September 1990, page 52

MTL seems to grow effortlessly year by year. The clear winner in 1990 was work on North Sea oil rigs, which accounted for around half UK turnover, in turn about a third of the total. Overseas trading saw good performances from newly established businesses in Australia and New Zealand and from India, where local manufacturing has begun. Profits also benefited from a £216,000 increase in interest receipts to £743,000.

"Good progress" is also forecast for 1991 and MTL's preliminary statement lists a number of products that have recently been launched. Trading may slow this year, but the group seems determined to maintain real returns of 12 per cent on sales and profits. **The shares are certainly not expensive.**

1. Positive Five Year Record

Earnings per share grew as follows:

1986	1987	1988	1989	1990
5.1p*	6.8p	8.6p	11.3p	13.7p

*Available from the offer document

You can readily see that earnings were increasing at over 20% per annum.

2. Low P/E Ratio in Relation to Growth Rate

At 150p the shares were priced at 11 times 1990 earnings and at 9.5 times the forecast for 1991. Earnings per share had grown at more than 20% compound since 1983, 21% in 1990, and the company was determined to grow at 12% in 'real terms' in 1991. With inflation running at 8.7% in March 1991 this could be interpreted as at least 20%.

3. Optimistic Chairman's Statement

In his statement the Chairman said that he was 'confident that MTL will continue to make good progress.' Brokers' forecasts, new product developments and an expanding market also supported his view.

4. Strong Liquidity, Low Borrowings and High Cash Flow

MTL enjoyed a superb financial position, with £4.7m net cash (equivalent to 18% of market capitalisation) and a strongly cash generative business.

5. Competitive Advantage

With 60% of the UK market and 25% of the world market, MTL could safely be said to have a powerful position in the niche industry of manufacturing intrinsic safety devices.

6. Something New

There was nothing 'new' except the company's innovative policy and a growing acceptance of the need for intrinsic safety. Given the company's very strong showing on all the other criteria, this was not a cause for concern.

7. Small Market Capitalisation

With the shares at 150p MTL was capitalised at £26.3m. Small enough to have been overlooked by institutions.

8. High Relative Strength

At 150p the shares were on their high.

9. Dividend Yield

Steadily rising dividends since one was first paid in 1988. The historic yield was an acceptable 2.5%.

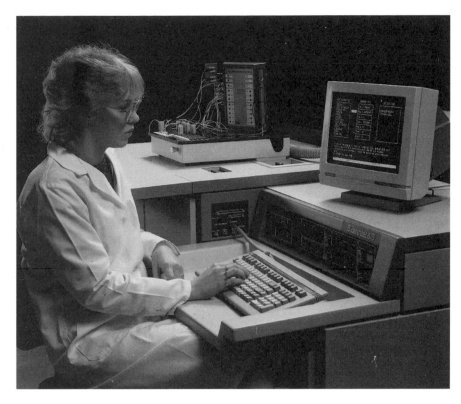

**TESTING AN MTL 825
MULTIPLEXER TRANSMITTER**

COURTESY OF MEASUREMENT
TECHNOLOGY LTD.

10. Reasonable Asset Position

Net assets per share stood at 52p, just over one third of the share price. Not very attractive in their own right, but passable for a growth share.

11. Management Shareholding

Directors, families and associates held 55.5% of the shares with a value of over £14.5m. Clearly the Directors could block a bid but they would certainly have the 'owner's eye'.

As you can see most of my criteria were well satisfied, the main exception being 'something new'. One year later, in March 1992, the shares had risen from 150p to 295p, giving a capital gain of 97% compared with the dismal performance of the market average of less than 5% during the same period. Increased earnings made a contribution to the gain but the major factor was the status change in the multiple.

MTL was an easy choice as most of my criteria were so obviously satisfied. Frequently, your decision will be much more difficult as your selection may not measure up on every count. You will need to know the criteria upon which you can place the most reliance and those that are less important. To this end, we must move on now from the stark outline I have given you to a much more detailed understanding of each of the criteria.

3

EARNINGS, GROWTH RATES AND THE PEG FACTOR

THE EARNINGS OF A COMPANY ARE THE NET PROFITS AFTER TAX ATTRIBUTABLE TO ORDINARY SHAREHOLDERS. If a company has earnings of 10p per share and a P/E ratio of 10, the shares would be priced at £1; with a P/E ratio of 20, the shares would be £2; and with a P/E ratio of 50 — £5. The annual rate of growth in earnings and the projected future rate of growth are the main factors which determine the multiple. The P/E ratio is the measure of how much you are paying for future growth and how much others have paid before you.

Earnings are the engine that drives the share price. If the engine fails or falters the shares will come down. The two charts overleaf show at a glance the close relationship between the earnings and the share prices of Glaxo and Hanson over the last fifteen years. There can be no doubt that earnings per share growth and the performance of share prices are umbilically linked, although there may be long periods during which they get out of kilter.

Very few companies can maintain a growth rate of over 30% per annum for more than a few years. The best bargains are usually found in the 15%-25% p.a. bracket. If you can identify a share growing at a sustainable rate of 20% p.a., it is almost beyond price. Even if you have to pay thirty times earnings, within five years earnings per share would have increased by 150%, and if the share price remained the same the

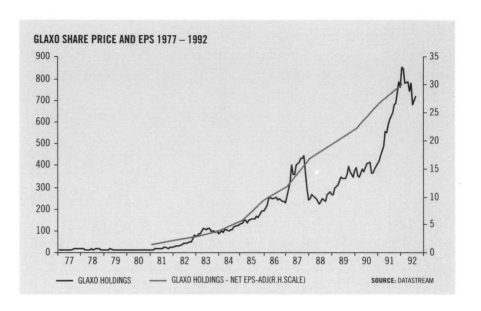

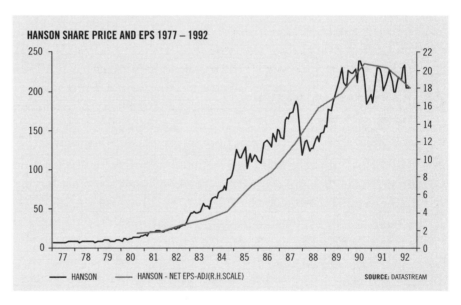

P/E ratio would have fallen to 12. In fact, all other things being equal, the P/E ratio for such a share would still be in the high 20s, so you would have at least doubled your money. You should also bear in mind that P/E ratios are usually higher in a non-inflationary climate. In times of lower interest rates the attractions of a share with a compound growth rate of 20% per annum are obviously much more apparent and contrast very favourably indeed with most alternative uses of money.

Let us examine how earnings per share have grown for the FT Ordinary Share Index during the last ten years. The average compound growth rate in earnings per share is about 10% per annum, whereas the average P/E ratio is approximately 11.7.

FT ORDINARY SHARE INDEX

Year ended 31st December	Closing level of Index	Historic PE ratio	EPS of Index	% Annual growth in EPS
1981	529	12.84	41.2	–
1982	589	10.95	53.8	+30.6
1983	773	13.00	59.5	+10.6
1984	945	10.35	91.3	+53.4
1985	1123	11.25	99.8	+9.3
1986	1272	11.76	108.2	+8.4
1987	1408	11.09	127.0	+17.4
1988	1447	9.44	153.3	+20.7
1989	1916	11.10	172.6	+12.6
1990	1687	10.18	165.7	-4.0
1991	1837	16.70	110.0	-33.6

SOURCE : DATASTREAM

The compounding effect of above average annual earnings growth is the vital factor that makes high-growth stocks so desirable. Here are a few typical growth rates within the range we are seeking:

COMPOUND INCREASE ON £100 INVESTED

	10%	15%	20%	25%	30%
Initial capital	£100	£100	£100	£100	£100
Year 1	110	115	120	125	130
Year 2	121	132	144	156	169
Year 3	133	152	173	195	220
Year 4	146	175	207	244	286
Year 5	161	201	249	305	371
Year 10	259	405	619	931	1379
Year 15	418	814	1541	2842	5119
Year 20	673	1637	3834	8674	19005
Year 25	1083	3292	9540	26470	70564

Clearly, the ideal investment is a company in which earnings per share are growing annually at a high and sustainable rate. If this kind of share can be purchased on a price earnings ratio below the market average, you have discovered a jewel beyond price. If the price earnings ratio is above the average of the market but modest in relation to the growth rate, you have still found a rare gem. Remember that there are only two basic reasons for a growth share appreciating in price. The first is earnings growth and the second is the increase in the multiple that the stockmarket awards to the company. The status change in the multiple can often be far more important than the growth in earnings.

To avoid paying an absurd price, I suggest that you use this check list first for measuring the P/E ratio of any share you are considering buying:

1. The past history of the P/E ratio for the company year by year indicates the level other investors believe to be normal.

2. The average P/E ratio for the industry. For an above average company you do not mind paying more, but not ridiculously so.

3. The average P/E ratio of the market as a whole is another basis for comparison. You know that your company is better than average but you do not intend to pay too much for the difference.

    Avoid stocks with astronomic ratings. Too many things can go wrong, and if anything does the fall will be catastrophic. Let me chill you with a look at some very high-multiple stockmarket favourites of yesteryear to see where they are today.

MIGHTY MULTIPLES OF THE PAST

USA Company	P/E Ratio Dec 1972	P/E Ratio May 1992
Sony	92	12
Polaroid	90	9
McDonalds	83	18
Baxter International	82	17
International Flavours	81	24
Automatic Data Processing	80	26

UK Company	July 1968	May 1992
Rank Organisation	46	22
General Electric	27	12
Tesco	43	14
Hanson (formerly Wiles Group)	27	12

As you can see, all of the companies that were so highly rated still exist but their multiples have had a reverse status change, especially in the USA where prospects are so often over-discounted.

After you check your selections against my three standards, I recommend you to take a very important additional measure. The P/E ratio can often simply be compared with the prospective growth rate. A company growing at 15% per annum should certainly command a P/E of 15; at 20% per annum a P/E of 20 and so on. By dividing the growth rate into the P/E ratio a price earnings growth factor (PEG) is established, *the aim being to find shares which have a PEG of well under one.*

Let us look at a few leading examples. Rentokil has been growing at a compound rate of approximately 20% per annum, and therefore for a company of such quality a prospective P/E ratio of about 20 would be justified. Unilever, growing at an average of about 11% per annum, commands a lower multiple in the region of 11.5. Both would have a PEG of about one. Another share might be on a multiple of 30 with a growth rate of only 20% per annum. The PEG would then be significantly over one at 1.5, and the share would be obviously expensive. Conversely, another share growing at 20% per annum on a multiple of only 10 would have a very attractive PEG of 0.5. Our target is a prospective PEG of not more than 0.75 and preferably less than 0.66. Put more simply, we want the multiple of estimated future earnings for the year ahead to be not more than three-quarters of the growth rate and preferably less than two-thirds.

You will remember the example of MTL in the previous chapter. The prospective multiple in March 1991 was about nine times estimated earnings for the year ahead. With an estimated growth rate of 20% per annum the prospective PEG was a very attractive 0.45.

At the lower levels of growth like 12.5% to 17.5% per annum the PEG formula works very well. At higher levels of growth you can stretch the P/E ratio a little. The reason for this is the compounding effect of earnings growing at an exceptional rate.

Let us look at three examples, small companies A,B and C, assuming that their share prices started at 100p and rose in line with earnings growing at 15%, 20% and 25% per annum respectively:

Year	A-15% p	B-20% p	C-25% p
1	115	120	125
2	132	144	156
3	152	173	195
4	175	207	244
5	201	249	305
10	405	619	931

As you can see, you would have made more money buying shares in company C than by investing in company A or company B. This assumes that all the companies remained on the same multiples. There would even be scope for the multiple of company C to drop from 25 to below 20.4 after five years or 16.6 after ten years before an investment in that company made less than an investment in company B.

I suggest that you stick with my rule-of-thumb measure and as a first step always simply compare the P/E ratio with the growth rate. The former should be less than three-quarters of the latter. You are seeking shares with a prospective PEG of not more than 0.75 and preferably under 0.66, but when the growth rate is at the high end of the range and all your other criteria are met, you can be a little more flexible.

Bear in mind that, all other things being equal, a share with a PEG of one is still a bargain. Over the last fifty years you would have fared exceptionally well by buying the market index on a PEG of one. However, you are not interested in the market as a whole — you are looking for the best shares within the market at absolutely bargain prices. Finding shares like these will ensure that you have the maximum chance of capital appreciation, and will at the same time provide you with an important safety factor. As we have seen, stocks with very high P/E ratios can fall a lot further than those on lower multiples.

Do not under-estimate the PEG factor as a measuring instrument and as a very important investment tool. Let me give you another example of how well it works in practice. In December 1990, *Analyst* recommended Domestic & General.

As you can see, there were excellent prospects for substantial growth in earnings per share. *Analyst's* estimate for 1991 was for an increase of 36.4% and for a further increase of 17.5% for 1992. The price in December 1990 was 363p giving an historic P/E ratio of 11.6 and a prospective P/E ratio of only 8.5 on a conservative view of future earnings growth of 20% per annum. Both the historic PEG and the prospective PEG were exceptionally attractive at 0.58 and 0.42 respectively.

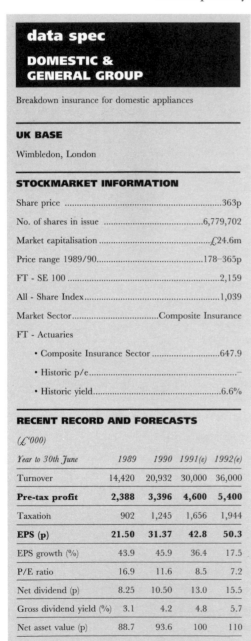

data spec
DOMESTIC & GENERAL GROUP

Breakdown insurance for domestic appliances

UK BASE

Wimbledon, London

STOCKMARKET INFORMATION

Share price	363p
No. of shares in issue	6,779,702
Market capitalisation	£24.6m
Price range 1989/90	178–365p
FT - SE 100	2,159
All - Share Index	1,039
Market Sector	Composite Insurance
FT - Actuaries	
• Composite Insurance Sector	647.9
• Historic p/e	—
• Historic yield	6.6%

RECENT RECORD AND FORECASTS

(£'000)

Year to 30th June	1989	1990	1991(e)	1992(e)
Turnover	14,420	20,932	30,000	36,000
Pre-tax profit	**2,388**	**3,396**	**4,600**	**5,400**
Taxation	902	1,245	1,656	1,944
EPS (p)	**21.50**	**31.37**	**42.8**	**50.3**
EPS growth (%)	43.9	45.9	36.4	17.5
P/E ratio	16.9	11.6	8.5	7.2
Net dividend (p)	8.25	10.50	13.0	15.5
Gross dividend yield (%)	3.1	4.2	4.8	5.7
Net asset value (p)	88.7	93.6	100	110

The calculations are very simple:

$$\frac{\text{P/E Ratio}}{\text{Estimated Growth Rate in Earnings Per Share}}$$

Historic PEG $=$ $\dfrac{11.6}{20}$ $=$ 0.58

Prospective PEG $=$ $\dfrac{8.5}{20}$ $=$ 0.42

By the end of 1991, the shares had soared from 363p to 1000p and the PEG had increased from 0.42 to 1.18 — still not expensive for such an exceptional growth share near to the end of its financial year. The 1992 prospective PEG would be at least 20% less and still be relatively attractive at under one. Note carefully that 70% (446p) of the increase in the share price from 363p to 1000p was due to the change in status —the change in the P/E ratio, not the increase in earnings per share.

HOWARD JAMES
MANAGING DIRECTOR,
DOMESTIC & GENERAL

You can see from these calculations that a critical factor is the estimated future growth rate. The past results are history but the future has to be a best guess. The Chairman's statement on the future outlook helps both at the year end and half-yearly. The 'body language' of the Chairman is also important. Be very wary if he sounds a note of caution. Furthermore, if the dividend has been increasing regularly, be on the alert if one year it is simply maintained.

The most reliable indicator for the future is probably the brokers' consensus estimate of future earnings. *The Estimate Directory* is an excellent publication which contains details of all brokers' estimates and your broker ought to have these at his fingertips. The important point about the consensus of brokers' estimates is that they are frequently based upon analysts' visits and should give you a very good feel for the future earnings potential of a company. Occasionally, you will be disappointed, but sometimes you may have a very happy surprise.

You should also be vigilant for press comment on anything the Chairman says at the AGM, to analysts or to the press throughout the year. Your broker should always let you know if there are any important developments, but not all announcements are given formally to the Stock Exchange. Most brokers subscribe to a press cuttings service. From time to time, it is worth checking with your broker to see if you have missed anything in the *Investors Chronicle*, *Financial Times* or the other newspapers and stockmarket newsletters that you read.

If you have invested in a company growing steadily each year, your main concern should be any slowing down in the rate of growth. There are few worse investments than a growth share going ex-growth. Any sign that the Chairman has become less optimistic or that things are not going according to plan will, almost certainly, be a good reason for you to sell your shares.

In the UK very few companies announce quarterly results. We have to rely upon half-yearly statements to measure progress and find out if there has been any variation in the earnings growth rate. Before making a final judgement, we must first make allowances for a few vital factors:

FAREPAK'S FARMHOUSE
HAMPER

1. Some businesses are highly seasonal — for example Farepak, a leading company in the hamper business, invariably reports a loss for the first half. The full year's results are made or broken by Christmas. You can only really compare the Christmas season with the previous one, and you need not be alarmed by losses in the first half.

    Many other businesses traditionally have a far better first half than second. This does not mean that their growth has slowed down; their business is similar to Farepak's but not so extreme. We deal with this reservation by simply comparing the current half year's results with those of exactly the same period in the previous year and the current year's results with those of previous years.

2. Some businesses are highly cyclical. These are not true growth shares, and will be subject to special consideration in Chapter Eleven. Some cycles last several years, so the increase in earnings during the up-period may seem like growth but, in reality, is simply the recovery from the previous cycle. Obvious examples of cyclical industries are house-building, car manufacture and distribution, timber and steel.

3. Allowance has to be made for times of deep recession. The niche businesses we are seeking will easily survive in these conditions, and most of them will continue to increase their earnings per share each year. However, there should be some tolerance for a diminution in the rate of growth during an extreme recessionary period.

You are seeking shares with an earnings growth rate of 15% per annum compound or more and a prospective PEG of not more than

0.75 and preferably less than 0.66. They are few and far between, but if you are selecting a team of cricket players you want a few stars like Botham and Gooch — not everyone who plays cricket. So be patient and keep looking until you find a share that really fits your criteria.

Remember that, ideally, you want there to be recent acceleration in the earnings growth rate. A company with a shorter record than five years might qualify, if there was new management with two or three years' evidence that substantial progress was being made. The key point is to look for companies that are still in a *dynamic* growth phase.

The New Issues market can be a very productive source for finding companies that are growing much faster than average. Take, for example, Sage, the computer software supplier which was floated in December 1989 at 130p per share on a prospective multiple of only seven times earnings. I kept an eye on Sage after the flotation and noticed how cheap the shares were when they were reviewed in the *Investors Chronicle* a year later.

Let us examine Sage in more detail. You will quickly see how well the statistics fulfilled my criteria:

1. Positive Five Year Record

Earnings per share grew as follows:

1986	1987	1988	1989	1990
2.6p	4.3p	6.7p	12.6p	19.2p

1990 was the first year as a public company but the *Investors Chronicle* article gave the full five year record. The earlier years would also be obtainable from the prospectus.

Although 1990 earnings did not increase at the same rate as the previous three years, 50% is still a phenomenal growth rate for a company of Sage's size.

2. Low P/E Ratio in Relation to Growth Rate

At 203p, the shares were priced at less than 11 times 1990 earnings and at less than 9 times estimated 1991 earnings. Although the growth rate looked like slowing to a more sustainable 25% per annum, the shares were still obviously very cheap with an historic PEG factor of only 0.44 and an astonishingly low prospective PEG factor of 0.36.

3. Optimistic Chairman's Statement

In December 1990, the Chairman said 'In the first two months of the current year, we have exceeded our internal targets. Despite the hostile business environment, we are confident that 1991 will be another year of continued growth.' You could hardly ask for more.

4. Strong Liquidity, Low Borrowings and High Cash Flow

Strong cash flow and £5.5m of net cash, amounting to 17% of market capitalisation, easily satisfied this criterion.

5. Competitive Advantage

A successful strategy coupled with a high level of advertising meant that Sage was continuing to increase market share and margins, despite very difficult conditions generally. Sage had about 40% of the market in small business software in the UK and was growing in the U.S. There were also many opportunities opening up in the Third World and Eastern Europe.

6. Something New

The financial difficulties being experienced by the company's main rival, Pegasus, were helping growth of market share in the U.K.

7. Small Market Capitalisation

At 203p the market capitalisation was a very attractive £33.1m.

8. High Relative Strength

The Datastream graph of relative performance against the FT-A All-Share Index is clearly very positive.

9. Dividend Yield

The yield was a very satisfactory 4.6%. 1990 was the first year a dividend was paid as a public company.

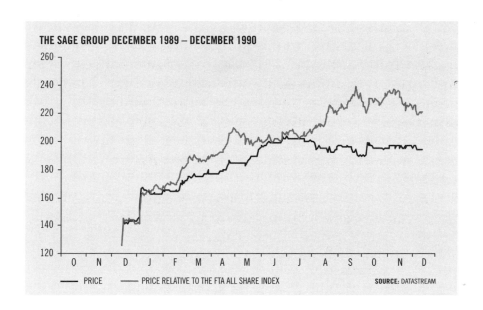

THE SAGE GROUP DECEMBER 1989 – DECEMBER 1990

— PRICE   — PRICE RELATIVE TO THE FTA ALL SHARE INDEX   **SOURCE:** DATASTREAM

10. Reasonable Asset Position

Negligible tangible assets, although £5.5m in net cash. The company also has valuable intellectual properties.

11. Management Shareholding

Directors owned 37% of the shares worth more than £12m, giving them the owner's eye.

Between December 1990 and May 1992, Sage shares rose from 203p to 469p, a gain of 131%, compared with the market average of 25%. Although Sage beat their forecast and earnings grew by a highly satisfactory 33% in 1991, the main contribution to the gain in the share price of 131% was the substantial increase in the company's multiple. The lower the prospective PEG at the time of purchase, the more scope there is for a dramatic upwards status change. The examples of Sage, Domestic & General and MTL Instruments illustrate how earnings growth and a status change in the multiple work in tandem to provide astute, systematic investors with exceptional gains. You can see how well the system works.

A further very important factor in buying a rapidly-growing stock, and in judging whether or not the P/E ratio is expensive, is the exact timing of your purchase. Let us return to MTL Instruments and assume that you had invested in the shares one month earlier. The price of the shares in February 1991 was 124p, and earnings per share in the last reported year to December 1989 were 11.3p. Therefore, you would have paid 11 times historic earnings and bought the shares on a prospective P/E ratio of 9 for the year ended December 1990. One month later in March 1991, the results for 1990 were announced. You would have known from the half year results that the profits were going to be excellent, but in February 1991 many investors were still valuing the shares on the historic multiple. The forecast for the following year, 1991, was optimistic, enabling analysts to estimate confidently that there would be a further 20% uplift in earnings. Within a few weeks the market began to think of the company on a prospective P/E ratio for 1991, which made the shares seem to be far cheaper than they were at the time of your purchase. When a baton is passed in a relay race attention focuses on the next runner and the next lap — moving from the historic to the prospective P/E ratio.

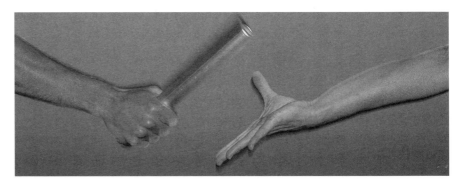

By purchasing *fast-growing* shares near the end of one financial year (or half year) you frequently enjoy a one-off gain as the market adjusts to absorb the results of the previous year and digests the news that next year should be even better. This process is aided by the press and by brokers, as relatively obscure companies receive very little press and broker comment throughout the year, often only having their moment in the sun when their results are announced.

A NUMBER OF POINTS IN THIS CHAPTER ARE WORTH REPEATING FOR BOTH EMPHASIS AND CLARIFICATION. YOU ARE SEEKING TO IDENTIFY SHARES WITH THE FOLLOWING CHARACTERISTICS:

1. Increased earnings per share over the last five years at a compound rate of about 15% per annum or more. A shorter period is

allowable when there is a recent acceleration in earnings, preferably with an easily identifiable and sustainable source such as new management.

2. A P/E ratio that is very attractive in relation to the growth rate with a target of a *prospective* PEG of not more than 0.75 and preferably under 0.66. Put another way, the prospective multiple should be not more than three-quarters of the estimated future growth rate and should preferably be under two-thirds.

3. A P/E ratio that is attractive in relation to the past history for the company, the average for the industry and the average for the market as a whole.

4. The chairman's yearly and half-yearly statements must be optimistic in tone and the dividend policy must be consistent with this. The market consensus of profit forecasts must also be optimistic.

OTHER IMPORTANT POINTS TO REMEMBER ARE:

1. The price of growth shares can only increase due to earnings growth and a status change in the multiple. The latter is often much more important than the former.

2. Avoid stocks on astronomic multiples.

3. When considering the half-yearly results pay particular attention to seasonal factors and bear in mind that some stocks traditionally have a better first six months.

4. Beware of confusing cyclical stocks in a recovery phase with growth stocks. Cyclical stocks are the subject of a separate system in a later chapter.

5. Fast-growing shares can often be purchased advantageously just before they announce their yearly or half-yearly results, when attention will shift from the historic to the prospective P/E ratio.

Now that you have a better understanding of earnings, growth rates and the PEG factor, we must spend some time on fine tuning.

4
—

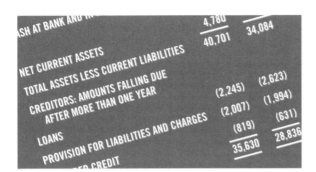

CREATIVE ACCOUNTING

IN THE LAST CHAPTER, I ELABORATED UPON THE FIRST THREE CRITERIA OF MY SYSTEM FOR INVESTING IN DYNAMIC GROWTH SHARES. To keep the explanations as simple as possible, I resisted the temptation of distracting you by suggesting that the earnings of a company may not be all that they appear. Now we come to fine tuning and must look at the dangers of taking annual earnings at their face value:

CREATIVE ACCOUNTING

Some members of the accountancy profession might argue that accounting is an exact science. Others see the presentation of Balance Sheets and Profit and Loss Accounts as more of an art form. Despite all the Institute of Chartered Accountants' recent efforts to improve accounting standards, there is still no doubt that a resourceful Finance Director has a considerable degree of flexibility in portraying his company's results. Financial creativity is easier in some industries than others, but in most businesses there is plenty of scope for an imaginative approach.

The Financial Reporting Council has stated that accounts should not only be true and fair but also informative. The Council goes on to say that no pressures can justify companies taking advantage of opportunistic developments in financial practice to window-dress accounts. The sentiment is laudable, but enforcement will be extremely difficult.

Various accounting bodies — the Accounting Standards Board (ASB), the Financial Reporting Council (FRC), the Financial Review Panel (FRP) and the Urgent Issues Task Force (UITF) — are working hard to improve standards, so this chapter might be a little out of date by the time you read these words. I can only give you a snapshot overview of the present position and make you aware of some of the problems you would have faced in June 1992 in determining, from a set of accounts, a true picture of the earnings growth of a company.

The simplest example of creative accounting is an invoice for services rendered which can be issued just after or just before the end of a financial year. As a result, profits will either be depressed or boosted according to the whim of the person making the decision.

Take another instance — a company in the building business which has an unsold house in the books at the end of its last financial year. The house could have been built during the first six months of the year at a cost of £100,000, and the estimated selling price might be £200,000. Accounting prudence demands that at the end of the year the house should be valued for accounting purposes at cost or market value whichever is the lower. On the first day of the current financial year, the house could be sold for the full asking price of £200,000 and alakazam, the profit of £100,000 would be brought into the current financial year, not the previous one. There is nothing sinister in this. The profit will not be made until the house is sold, but one day can make all the difference to the annual profits. You can readily see that many an entrepreneur anxious to preserve his company's unbroken record of earnings per share growth would make every effort to sell the house in a year in which profits were poor. Conversely, if business had been excellent and the future outlook appeared murky, our entrepreneur might deliberately delay a sale by a few days to swing the profits into the more difficult period ahead. I have illustrated my point with only one house but there could be many. In some businesses, several million pounds could easily be shunted from one financial year to another with this kind of approach.

Provisions are another area which offer scope for transferring profits to another year. Let us assume that our entrepreneur has had a good year and wants to tune down his company's profits a little. When reviewing the outstanding debtors he simply decides to adopt an exceptionally cautious view over the amount to be provided for bad debts.

Unless he is blatantly and obviously wrong, the auditors are unlikely to challenge his prudence. Similarly, he might argue that a more substantial provision should be made against the value of old stock and work in progress. These simple examples show how profits can be transferred from one year to another either intentionally or fortuitously.

Any qualification of the Auditor's Report can be a sign that the company is heading for trouble. You must also be on the alert for proposed changes in the company's auditor, especially from a leading firm to a small and obscure one. These are obvious warning signals; more subtle ones emerge from studying the methods some companies use in other areas of accounting that lend themselves to inventive treatment:

a) Research and Development Costs

Development costs may be deferred to future periods in respect of defined projects, the outcome of which can be assessed with reasonable certainty as to their technical feasibility and commercial viability. Otherwise all research and development costs should be written off in the financial period during which they are incurred.

This is the guidance given in Statement of Standard Accounting Practice (SSAP) 13, which goes a long way towards preventing manipulation of Research and Development costs between one year and the next. However, even this kind of definition cannot be sufficiently precise. The words 'reasonable certainty as to their technical feasibility' offer scope for an opinion as to what is or is not 'reasonable'. The final view could easily be coloured by an entrepreneur trying to improve profits or hold them back.

b) Advertising Expenditure

In June 1992, there was no SSAP or other definitive guideline about the treatment of advertising expenditure. The normal conservative accounting approach is to write off the expenditure as incurred. An equally acceptable alternative in the case of a major campaign for a new product is to write off the expenditure over several years. The Finance Director's opinion is all-important. He in turn has to persuade the auditors that his ideas are correct. Any unusual treatment would have to be disclosed in the Accounts. On this subject, companies often have very different accounting policies so investors should read the detailed Notes to the Accounts very carefully.

c) Currency Fluctuations

ASIL NADIR
FORMER CHAIRMAN, POLLY PECK

Polly Peck was the most notorious perpetrator of boosting profits with currency transactions. A large amount of money was borrowed in hard currency like Swiss francs at a cost of say 7% per annum, and invested at a much higher rate of say 20% in a weak currency. The difference of 13% per annum was brought into the accounts as a profit. On the other side of the coin, the weak currency depreciated in value during the year by say 15%, but this was shown as a reduction of capital in the Balance Sheet. There was a note in the Annual Report under the heading of Accounting Policies stating that 'The effect of variances in the exchange rates between the beginning and end of the financial year on the net investment in subsidiary companies is dealt with through reserves.' Easy to see with hindsight.

d) Re-organisation Expenses

The UITF has recommended that re-organisation costs should in future be presented as exceptional, and charged against earnings per share, unless they result from the closure of a segment of a special part of the business sufficiently large to have its own management accounts. Previously, re-organisation costs could be written off as an extraordinary item, with the result that earnings per share were not affected.

Conglomerates and acquisitive companies (one of which I managed for a while!) have taken advantage of the earlier rules by making massive provisions for *future* re-organisation costs. These were shown as an extraordinary item, as they were for *future* costs which obviously could not be charged against the current year and would be difficult to allocate against individual future years. The effect of making too large a provision for future costs was, of course, to increase future revenue profits. Many future expenses could easily be classified as part of the re-organisation and charged against the provision instead of the year's profits.

e) Methods of Stock Valuation

Last-in-first-out (LIFO) is more conservative in inflationary times than first-in-first-out (FIFO). A change of method will be highlighted in the accounts and the effect should be noted carefully.

f) Changes in Method of Depreciation

Some methods are faster than others, so always look to see if there is a change and whether or not the company's earnings have obviously benefited as a result. In the year of the change this should be easy to spot.

g) Sale of Fixed Assets

The profit or loss on the sale of a fixed asset is part of the company's ordinary operations. If particularly large, it should be shown as exceptional. A profit or loss arising on the sale of a business or part of a business is also now regarded as an exceptional item and should be taken into account in calculating earnings per share. You will have to make your own judgement on whether or not you consider such a profit or loss to be a true part of the company's earnings for the year in question.

h) Capitalisation of Interest

Normally interest is charged against profit, but on occasions the interest cost of a particular project is added to the capital cost. The use of this technique flatters both the asset value in the Balance Sheet and the profits in the Profit and Loss Account. Obviously, there is considerable scope for abuse, especially by over-geared property companies anxious to reassure their bankers and loan stockholders.

i) Earn-Outs

Companies frequently finance acquisitions by making a down-payment to be supplemented by a subsequent payment, in either shares or cash, based upon a multiple of profits to be made during the next few years. The future liability is not usually shown clearly in the accounts and in earnings per share calculations. If the share price has fallen drastically by the time the final payment is due, this can result in very substantial dilution. In these circumstances, any heavy cash liability might also be difficult to fund.

Potential liabilities for deferred consideration will be shown in the Notes to the Accounts under a heading of that name, Financial Commitments, Contingent Liabilities or something similar. Be vigilant!

j) Change of Financial Year End

By changing a financial period, year to year comparison of earnings growth is made more difficult. With most companies there will be a good reason for doing so but on occasions the motive might be more covert. You must be alert to this possibility.

Your main concern is to try to establish the annual growth rate of a company's earnings per share. Extraordinary and exceptional charges muddy the water and make an analyst's task far more difficult. Almost all of these are part of the cost of being in business. A strike or a very large, unexpected bad debt might be classified as exceptional, but strikes and bad debts happen in business very frequently indeed.

Before you accept the earnings per share figure, you must examine each exceptional item in detail to see if any profits should be eliminated. You should also look at the items charged as exceptional expenses in case any of them should be added back to increase profits.

Extraordinary items should become very rare under the proposed new recommendations outlined in a Financial Reporting Exposure Draft (FRED 1). Major changes in the format of the Profit and Loss Account are also proposed. If adopted as a new standard, group accounts would have to separate the results of continuing operations from discontinued ones; segregate acquisitions and unusual items; abolish extraordinary items in almost all cases; explain reserve movements; and disclose revenue investment. Extraordinary items are now defined as those which derive from rare events or transactions that fall outside the ordinary activities of the company. A further important proposal in FRED 1 is that earnings per share should be calculated *after* extraordinary items, which should be disclosed on the face of the Profit and Loss Account. Companies may also show earnings per share calculated in a different way, provided the basis is consistent, clearly explained and reconciled with the earnings presentation proposed by FRED 1. In other words, the Directors can attempt to show a truer earnings picture for the year, provided they explain exactly what they are doing.

There are substantial differences in accounting standards between the UK and the US. Standard setting in the US began in 1930 whilst in the UK the accountancy bodies only began issuing SSAPs in 1970. The US standards cover practically all conceivable accounting alternatives and have been recognised as authoritative by the SEC and the US courts. In the UK, it is only since the formation of the ASB in 1990 that standards have begun to have statutory implications. Directors can now be forced to pay for the reissue of accounts that do not meet the required accounting standards. Board members beware - the ASB is looking for scalps!

Where does all this leave the investor? The rules of the game are being tightened, but meanwhile you have to make judgements of earnings per share and growth rates. How extraordinary is extraordinary, and how exceptional is exceptional must be your constant questions. Earnings per share will in future be shown after extraordinary and exceptional items, which will be clearly explained. Your task will be to decide if any of them should be added back or eliminated to give you a truer picture of the growth prospects.

Ben Graham, the well-known American investor, suggested that auditors should make their best guess for apportioning exceptional items over a period of years. In this way, earnings per share would be much more related to individual years and growth would be easier to calculate. Graham also suggested taking the average of the last three years' adjusted earnings and comparing them with the average of another three year tranche of adjusted earnings from say five or ten years earlier. This would help to smooth out the effect of extraordinary and exceptional items. Certainly, there is something to be said for working on averages, especially for conglomerates and other highly acquisitive companies.

"Creative accounting — and you?"

One of the most reliable cross-checks on earnings is a company's cash flow during the same period. In 1991, for instance, ICI had trading profits of £1bn and excellent operating cash flow of £1.5bn. In contrast, British Aerospace had profits before tax and exceptional items of £154m, and operating cash inflow of minus £95m. A prize also goes to Polly Peck, which in its farewell set of accounts showed pre-tax profits up 44% at £161m — but in the new style of cash flow statements, County Nat West calculated that the operating cash *outflow* would have been £129m. The main reason was a staggering increase in working capital of £288m. When there is a large divergence the wrong way, you will know that creative accounting has been at work.

Whatever else you do, keep an eye open for profit boosting by the methods I have mentioned, cross-check with cash flow and always read the annual report and accounts from beginning to end. Remember that footnote 34 (d) or even 63 (c) might contain a very important message for you.

CONVERTIBLES

Any calculation of earnings per share should allow for convertible loan stocks, bonds and preference shares being converted and options and warrants being exercised. Where these total less than 10% of the shares in issue, they are not worth complicating your thinking, so I suggest that you ignore them. The conversion of a loan will save some interest, and the exercise of warrants or options will bring fresh cash into the company. There would be a little dilution of earnings but not enough to worry about.

Occasionally, a company has a massive convertible which definitely distorts the earnings picture and cannot be ignored. For example, in April 1990, Owners Abroad took over Redwing Holidays from British Airways and issued a convertible for £17.25m to fund the purchase. By the end of 1990, Owners Abroad had over 27 million of the convertible preference shares in issue. At a conversion price equivalent to 65p a share they would convert into just over 41.7 million ordinary shares (153 ordinary shares for every 100 convertibles) between April 1991 and the year 2000. To calculate maximum potential dilution, you have to assume that all will be converted. You therefore add the 41.7 million potential additional ordinary shares for conversion of the preference shares to the 5.95 million for options, and add the total to the average number of shares in issue during the year. In this case, the increase would be just under 40%.

For a rough guide to see how this would affect earnings per share, you simply divide the new total into forecast profits after tax. However, for a more accurate result, you should take into account the potential dividend or interest saving, as the company, after conversion, will no longer have to pay the preference dividend or loan stock interest.

Fortunately the calculations are usually made for you. All the options and convertibles are shown in the Notes to the Accounts under the heading of Called-up Share Capital or something similar, and the potential effect of reinvesting the proceeds is shown under Earnings Per Share.

As you can see, dilution can turn out to be significant with a consequent depressing effect on the growth of earnings per share. When the number of shares to be issued on conversion is more than 10% of share capital, you should make the necessary calculations to gauge the effect. Needless to say, the lower the conversion price, the more likely it is that convertibles will be converted.

TAXATION

Frequently, companies have tax losses brought forward and available to set off against current profits. This can result in an abnormally low tax charge for the year during which the tax loss is used. Earnings per share growth is based upon earnings after tax. The tax charge should therefore be adjusted back to a normal level to obtain a true picture. Companies operating in enterprise zones and companies in Ireland often enjoy tax breaks and receive capital grants. Heavy capital expenditure in some engineering and leasing companies also lowers the tax charge. You should adjust the tax charge to a normal level if the tax break is unlikely to recur.

Take a company with a normal tax rate of say 33.3%. If profits before tax were £12m and net earnings after tax were £10m, that would mean that for some reason the tax charge had been reduced to only 16.7%. If this exceptionally low tax charge appeared to be due to a one-off happening, you would simply deduct 33.3% from pre-tax profits of £12m, to give you revised net profits of £8m upon which to base your earnings per share calculations.

It is very important to distinguish between companies that regularly pay lower tax and those that have benefited from an isolated, non-recurring event.

LET ME SUMMARISE FOR YOU THE MAIN POINTS THAT HAVE BEEN MADE IN THIS CHAPTER:

1. The accountancy profession is putting its house in order, but there will always be scope for creative accounting.

2. You must make a point of reading the detailed notes to the Report and Accounts as well as the Chairman's Statement. Read all documents you receive from your selected companies from cover to cover. Be on the alert for warning signals, especially qualifications of the Auditor's Report or a proposed change of auditor.

3. Earnings per share will in future be shown after extraordinary and exceptional items which will be clearly explained. Your task must be to decide if any of them should be added back or eliminated to give you a truer picture of the company's growth prospects.

4. Keep your eye open for profit-boosting by the methods I have outlined. *Your best cross-check is to compare trading profits with operating cash flow.* Any large divergence between the two will warn you that creative accounting may have been at work.

5. Whenever convertibles, options and warrants total more than 10% of the share capital, adjust earnings figures by assuming dilution and potential interest savings.

6. With acquisitive companies make sure by studying the Notes to the Accounts that the liabilities for deferred consideration on earn-outs have not become excessively onerous.

7. Adjust earnings to allow for a normal tax charge if the tax for the year has been reduced as a result of a non-recurring event.

We can now move on to the first of my protective criteria, which, taken together, will form a safety net under any shares you buy.

Postscript — Since writing this chapter, an excellent book on the subject of creative accounting has been published. *Accounting for Growth* by Terry Smith gives, among other things, a comprehensive account of the many ways of boosting a company's earnings per share growth. If you are seriously interested in mastering the complexities of company accounting, you should read this book.

5

LIQUIDITY, CASH FLOW AND BORROWINGS

I COULD HAVE SIMPLY ENTITLED THIS CHAPTER 'A STRONG FINANCIAL POSITION' BUT I WANTED TO HIGHLIGHT LIQUIDITY, CASH FLOW AND BORROWINGS AS THREE VERY IMPORTANT AND DISTINCT FACTORS.

The word 'liquidity' refers to assets that are 'easily converted into cash'. The assets in question are usually short-term loans, debtors (less creditors), gilts, quoted investments and, of course, cash. The word 'easily' means 'free of pain or trouble'. In a deep recession, debtors could be much more difficult to convert than you might expect (ask any bank) but we will proceed on the basis that the financial climate is reasonably normal.

Obviously, a company is in a strong financial position if it has substantial cash balances and no debt. Provided that the strong liquid position has been achieved by organic growth, this must be taken as excellent prima facie evidence that the company is a cash generator of a high order.

Now let us look at a less fortunate company with cash balances of say £1m but debt of £5m. We will assume that the £1m has not arisen from a recent rights issue or other funding of a similar nature. The key questions are: how pressing is the debt, and is the company truly a cash generator? The debt will be classified in the accounts between that falling due within one year and longer term obligations. In this case there might be an overdraft of £1m and a mortgage on the company's main property of £4m. If the mortgage is short-term you might decide to move on to another company, but if it is long-term your due diligence should continue.

Another useful way of checking a company's soundness is the 'quick ratio' of current assets, less stocks and work in progress, to current liabilities. I like to see current assets less stocks at least 1.5 times current liabilities, but I would accept less (possibly down to 1:1) if everything else seemed to be in order. The higher the ratio the better. You will discover later when reading Chapter Thirteen on 'Value Investing' that Ben Graham's disciples' main criterion used to be finding companies selling at a discount to their net current asset values. There are very few of these around nowadays, but a strong net current asset position is a highly desirable investment criterion to add to your repertoire and strengthen your safety net.

Another useful measure is the overall debt to equity ratio of a company. Equity in this case is the net asset value attributable to ordinary shareholders. This sounds simple, but beware — professional investors seem to have many different interpretations of the meaning of the words 'net asset value' and 'overall debt'. My method is a harsh one by some standards — I only take the tangible assets, so I deduct goodwill from the total balance sheet figure. To calculate overall debt, I add all the creditors of over one year to the bank overdraft, add any short-term loans and hire purchase and finance lease obligations; then I deduct surplus cash and express the resultant total as a percentage of the net tangible assets. Let me show you how this worked with a May 1992 new issue, Industrial Control Services Group plc.

First turn to the pro-forma balance sheet, which shows net assets after the placing of £17,116,000. Deduct intangible assets of £472,000 to give net tangible assets of £16,644,000. Now take all interest-bearing liabilities falling due after more than one year, £6,350,000 (£6,564,000 less £214,000 accruals) — this figure includes mortgages together with some finance leases and hire purchase obligations. Then turn to creditors falling due within one year (see overleaf) and extract interest-bearing current instalments on bank loan of £64,000, bank overdraft of £6,054,000, other loans of £1,000,000 and hire purchase contracts of £331,000. The total of these figures is £7,449,000, from which you should deduct cash in the pro-forma balance sheet of £6,104,000 and the £1,000,000 that has been repaid to creditors after the placing. The

INDUSTRIAL CONTROL SERVICES GROUP PLC
PRO FORMA BALANCE SHEET

	30th Nov 1991 (£'000)	Capital reorganisation (£'000)	Placing (£'000)	Pro forma total (£'000)
Fixed assets				
Intangible assets	472	-	-	472
Tangible assets	12,282	-	-	12,282
Investments	695	-	-	695
	13,449	-	-	13,449
Current assets				
Stocks	6,684	-	-	6,684
Debtors	20,183	-	-	20,183
Cash at bank and in hand	379	125	5,600	6,104
	27,246	125	5,600	32,971
Creditors				
Amounts falling due within one year	23,553	-	(1,000)	22,553
Net current assets	3,693	125	6,600	10,418
Total assets less current liabilities	17,142	125	6,600	23,867
Creditors				
Amounts falling due after more than one year	6,564	-	-	6,564
Provisions				
Deferred taxation	225	-	-	225
Minority interests	(38)	-	-	(38)
	6,751	-	-	6,751
Net assets employed	10,391	125	6,600	17,116
Capital and reserves				
Called up share capital	4,500	(1,192)	682	3,990
Share premium account	-	210	5,918	6,128
Profit and loss account	4,946	(250)	-	4,696
Capital reserve	3	-	-	3
Capital redemption reserve	-	1,357	-	1,357
Intangibles reserve	(1,959)	-	-	(1,959)
Revaluation reserve	2,901	-	-	2,901
	10,391	125	6,600	17,116

The following pro forma balance sheet of the ICS Group is provided for illustrative purposes only and is based on the audited consolidated balance sheet of the Group at 30th November, 1991 adjusted as set out in the notes below.

Notes

1 Adjustments have been made to reflect the special resolution passed on 18th May, 1992 to reorganise the share capital of the Group and the exercise of the share warrant by 3i. For further details see paragraphs 1.3 and 1.4 of the section headed "Further information" on page 49.

2 It is assumed that the placing proceeds net of expenses will be £6.6m.

3 The impact of the results of the Group after 30th November, 1991 has not been taken into account.

INDUSTRIAL CONTROL SERVICES GROUP PLC
CREDITORS: AMOUNTS FALLING DUE WITHIN ONE YEAR

	31st May 1991 (£000)	30th November 1991 (£000)
Current instalments on bank loan	60	64
Other loans	-	1,000
Bank overdraft	3,149	6,054
Dividend payable	108	162
Obligations under finance leases and hire purchase contracts (see note 16)	186	331
Trade creditors	7,323	6,129
Contract payments on account	1,154	2,478
Other creditors	920	479
Current corporation tax	1,386	1,731
Other taxes and social security costs	1,249	1,351
Accruals and deferred income	3,290	3,774
	18,825	23,553

The bank overdraft is secured by first fixed and floating charges over all the assets of the group.

INDUSTRIAL CONTROL SERVICES GROUP PLC
CREDITORS: AMOUNTS FALLING DUE AFTER MORE THAN ONE YEAR

	31st May 1991 (£000)	30th November 1991 (£000)
Bank loans at variable interest rates repayable within five years	119	77
Mortgages at variable interest rates repayable within twenty years by the proceeds of endowment policies	4,000	4,000
Mortgages at variable interest rates repayable within five years	1,400	1,400
Obligations under finance leases and hire purchase contracts (see note 16)	485	873
Other loans at variable interest rates repayable within five years	1,000	-
Accruals and deferred income	303	214
	7,307	6,564

resultant figure is £345,000, which added to the £6,350,000 of creditors due after one year gives 'overall debt'* of £6,695,000. The percentage of net debt to equity is calculated as follows:-

$$\frac{6,695,000}{16,644,000} \quad x \quad 100 \quad = \quad 40.2\%$$

My limit for growth companies is 50% so this is just acceptable.

* 'OVERALL DEBT' FROM PREVIOUS PAGE

There seem to be several other anomalies in calculating net debt. For example, I would have thought that a dividend due within a month of the accounts being published should also be classified as debt. The payment will increase the overdraft or reduce the cash balance so if the snapshot was to be taken only one month later, debt would undoubtedly be higher. Similar remarks apply to the tax liability, although this would not have to be paid so quickly. When I stop to think about this problem, I also wonder about capital commitments which will in some cases soon become part of overall debt. If you really want to get down to fine tuning you have to be aware of all of these points, but to keep your approach simple I suggest that you only bother about them when the overall debt figure is marginal and you are beginning to feel uneasy about the company.

Another contentious area seems to be convertibles. If the share price is well above the conversion price there is an argument for ignoring them when calculating overall debt, especially if the conversion date is near. If the conversion price is miles above the share price, the convertible must be classified as debt, as any Ratners shareholder will confirm. In the middle ground, when the share price is near to the conversion price, the prudent course is to classify the convertible as debt.

You need not worry too much about having to make the calculation of the net debt percentage. The *Investors Chronicle* adopts a similar method to mine and always highlights the figure in its reviews of company results.

Ideally, we are seeking growth companies with net cash, so remember that any debt is already the beginning of a compromise. Up to a 50% net debt position can be tolerated if all of our other investment criteria are well and truly satisfied.

Occasionally, you will be unintentionally misled by companies that are in businesses like construction which receive large deposits in advance of major contracts. I remember that Whessoe, for example, had a rights issue in 1991 to fund an overseas acquisition. Although the company seemed to have a strong cash position at the time, the board rightly pointed out to shareholders that much of their cash was not free as it represented deposits made by customers in advance of substantial contracts.

Moving on now from the present position of a company to future cash flow, we need first to define the term. Cash flow is the net amount of money a company generates during its financial year. To calculate net cash flow, you add back to the net trading profits those items requiring no cash outlay. The main one is of course depreciation.

Conversely, the profit retained by an associate company that has been equity accounted has to be deducted from net trading profits. For example, if the company under review held 20%, with board representation of an associate which had made a profit of £10m after tax, the annual net profits figure of the group would include a pro rata contribution of £2m. The associate may, however, only have paid a dividend of a quarter of that amount, and therefore in cash terms only £500,000 would have been received. The retained balance of £1.5m would have to be deducted from profits to determine the operating net cash flow for the year.

In an attempt to make the investor's task easier, the Accounting Standards Board now has a new mandatory requirement for a Cash Flow Statement in place of the old Statement of Sources and Applications of Funds. The new statement splits cash flow into different categories and attempts to classify sources of movements into their economic causes. Future headings will be: net cash inflow from operating activities, returns on investments and servicing of finance, taxation, investing and financing. There is a mass of figures, so focus upon the most important single point — *the net cash inflow from operating activities should not be materially different from the profit arising from trading operations.*The accounts of Sainsbury for the 52 weeks to 14th March 1992 illustrate very clearly how easy it is to reconcile operating profits with net cash inflow from operating activities. In the Group Cash Flow Statement you are immediately referred to Note 24 which is set out below:

Note 24
RECONCILIATION OF OPERATING PROFIT TO NET CASH INFLOW FROM OPERATING ACTIVITIES

	Group	
	1992	*1991*
	£m	*£m*
Operating profit	**667.7**	585.0
Profit sharing	**(49.4)**	(44.0)
Depreciation charges	**135.6**	120.2
Increase in stocks	**(1.5)**	(52.3)
Decrease (Increase) in debtors	**4.7**	(9.7)
Increase in creditors	**31.7**	109.2
Net cash inflow from operating activities	**788.8**	708.4

As you can see the Operating Profit is £667.7m from which £49.4m is deducted for the retail employees Profit Sharing Scheme. There is then a very substantial £135.6m added back for Depreciation which, although charged against profits, does not absorb cash. The rest of the adjustments are related to working capital requirements — increases or decreases in stocks, debtors and creditors.

The final result is a healthy £788.8m *net cash inflow from operating activities,* which compares very favourably with the £667.7m of *operating profit.* Many Reports and Accounts are not as well set out as Sainsbury's. The less clear they are the more vigilant you should be. Concentrate upon the key figures. *When operating profit exceeds net cash inflow from operating activities,* you know that creative accounting has almost certainly been at work.

Why is cash flow so important? First, as a check that trading profits and therefore earnings are in order, and second, because free cash flow funds the expansion of a company. By the term 'free cash flow' I mean cash flow after dividends and after capital expenditure. Good examples of businesses with excellent cash flow are food retailers like Sainsbury or Tesco. They need very little capital to open a new supermarket — the property can be rented and stocks of food financed by suppliers. From the opening day the tills ring up disposable cash. Bread, for example, is supplied on credit by the bakers, sold for cash and eaten within a day or so. A few weeks and in some cases months later, the baker's account is settled by the supermarket, which has enjoyed the use of the cash in the meantime. At the end of its financial year the cash profits of a supermarket are spent on taxes, dividends, the repayment of debt and of course on new supermarkets to generate further growth. The only worry is when over-expansion and over-building causes conditions to become so competitive that there is a price war. They rarely last for long though — why spoil a good thing?

I was never quite sure why Jimmy Goldsmith attached so much importance to brand names like Bovril and Marmite, and why when making his early fortune, he concentrated upon food retailing with Allied Suppliers in the UK and Grand Union in America. I have now caught up with his thinking. I hope to show you how to invest in companies like these — companies that enjoy a competitive advantage, a high rate of return on capital employed and a strong cash flow, which is not eaten up by capital commitments of a negative kind.

Capital expenditure falls into two main categories. The first is the replacement of an old asset such as plant and machinery, which is in a bad state of repair or has become obsolete. This is more in the nature of maintaining the status quo — an essential cost to stay competitive. The second category of capital expenditure is far more up-beat — a brand new, additional factory, together with the most modern equipment — the stuff that makes for real expansion. You will find that there are some businesses, like steel companies, that have to invest every year in plant and equipment. Their shareholders rarely benefit.

Companies with very strong business franchises are more fortunate.

They can invest in new products, new technology and new businesses, all of which should help to increase, *as opposed to maintain*, annual profits.

THESE ARE THE CONCLUSIONS WE HAVE REACHED

1. The ideal company, particularly in recessionary times, is one with high net cash flow, substantial cash balances and no debt.

2. Our outside limit for borrowings is 50% of net assets and this is only if all other criteria are very much in place.

3. The quick ratio of net current assets, less stocks and work in progress, to current liabilities should be at least 1:1 and preferably 1.5:1.

4. An eye must be kept open for distorted cash positions in contracting companies, which often have substantial deposits from customers paid in advance.

5. The Cash Flow Statement of a company should always be studied. *In particular, double-check that the net operating cash flow is at least the same, and preferably more, than the net operating profits.* If there is a material discrepancy the wrong way, creative accounting has been at work.

6. Companies that need to spend heavily on capital equipment simply to stay alive should be avoided. Companies which generate plenty of *free* cash flow to expand future earnings are far more attractive.

6

SOMETHING NEW

SOMETHING NEW IS A HIGHLY DESIRABLE BUT NOT ABSOLUTELY MANDATORY CRITERION FOR INVESTMENT. Companies with excellent brand names, like Glaxo and Cadbury Schweppes, and well established companies in niche markets like Rentokil, continue to churn out increased earnings per share at well above average rates year in and year out without the benefit of anything new. They may add a new product or service to their range, but nothing dramatic — nothing that in itself would cause earnings to soar. Knowing that I might find another growth share like Glaxo or Rentokil, I do not insist upon any new selection of mine benefiting from something new, provided that most of my other investment criteria are met. However, when I do find a share that has all the right fundamentals and the added advantage of something new, that really gets my taste buds going. So often, the new event or product is a wonderful confirmatory bonus explaining the increased earnings potential and high relative strength of the shares.

There are four main categories of new factors which are of sufficient importance to have a major impact upon share prices:

1.   NEW MANAGEMENT.

2.   NEW PRODUCTS OR TECHNOLOGY.

3.   NEW EVENTS IN THE INDUSTRY AS A WHOLE, INCLUDING NEW LEGISLATION.

4.   NEW ACQUISITIONS.

New management is the most important of all. The reason is simple — the impact of excellent new management can be both far-reaching and on-going. If new managers of calibre take control of a company, their efforts are likely to bear fruit for many years to come.

Two of the many well-known examples are James Hanson and Gordon White, who joined the board of Wiles Group, and Greg Hutchings, a senior executive of Hanson who joined F.H.Tomkins. The Wiles Group became Hanson and has grown from under £2m to over £11bn during the following twenty-eight years; Tomkins has grown from £6m to £1.4bn during the nine years since the arrival of Greg Hutchings. The benefits of these management changes continued for many years and are still continuing today.

The gains from a new product or new technology can also be on-going. For example, in October 1981, Glaxo launched a new patented product, Zantac, for the treatment of ulcers. By 1991, the sales of Zantac totalled £1.6bn. At the time of the launch, it would have been difficult to anticipate the worldwide success of Zantac, but shortly after 1983, when the product was approved for use in America and broke all records for a new drug there, any intelligent investor could have enjoyed a massive capital gain. The sales of Zantac are levelling off now but the product continues to make a major contribution to Glaxo's profits.

Psion's new palm-top computer, the award winning star of a leading international computer show in America in 1991, should have a major impact upon Psion's future sales and profits. However, in the fast moving computer industry there will always be the worry of a competitor developing something better. Products of this kind are hard to patent and the key factor is the length of lead time. Companies like Psion have to make hay while the sun shines. It is important for you to distinguish between patented new products and those that can be more easily displaced by market forces.

Sometimes a new product might be a tremendous success but will

GLAXO SHARE PRICE (£)

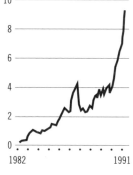

ZANTAC SALES (£'m)

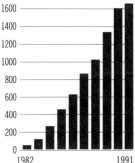

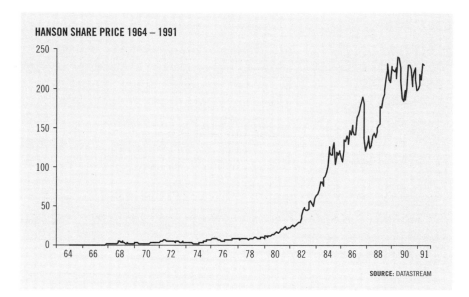

HANSON SHARE PRICE 1964 – 1991

SOURCE: DATASTREAM

TOMKINS SHARE PRICE 1983 – 1992

SOURCE: DATASTREAM

LORD HANSON

LORD WHITE

GREG HUTCHINGS

have little impact upon the company's earnings due to the relative unimportance of the new product within the group. I am sure that Sony benefited from the Walkman, but the success of that product did not transform Sony's already massive profits. In contrast, Nintendo benefited far more directly from the success of its video games. Your task is to use your best judgement to determine whether or not a new product will be a winner and to evaluate its likely effect upon a company's earnings. This is not always easy, so I suggest that when looking for something new you only consider products that obviously constitute a substantial proportion of the company's business, are central to the main activity and will have a major impact upon future earnings. For example, Polaroid in America had one of the best new ideas of this century with a new instantly developed photograph. The company subsequently invented a colour version and as a result in the sixties the stock multiplied in value many times. A good proportion of the world's population must have realised that Polaroid had something new, that it was a major part of their business and that earnings would benefit for many years to come.

The other consideration for a new product is to distinguish between gimmicks that will have a short life and those that might last indefinitely. In the toy industry Barbie has been alive and well for fifty years, but the Wombles of Wimbledon are now long forgotten. Teenage Mutant Ninja Turtles are one of the latest crazes, but I would not award them a high multiple.

New events in an industry would of course include the collapse of a main competitor. The failure of Harry Goodman's International Leisure Group made life easy for Owners Abroad, Airtours and the rest of the holiday business. The finding of oil in the North Sea obviously benefited many oil rig suppliers and property and service businesses in the City of Aberdeen. Wars benefit companies in the defence industry. A change of government could influence the future level of spending on hospitals, and fresh legislation on the disposal of waste and the cleaning up of the environment could have far reaching effects upon companies connected with that industry. The planned opening of the Channel Tunnel has already been a major influence upon the value of property in Northern France and the South of England. German reunification gave a massive boost to consumer demand benefiting most of West German industry, especially automobile manufacturers. There are hundreds of other examples.

From now on try to think about events in this way. As you read the details of a major new development or product, make a conscious effort to decide whether or not it is likely to be a long-term winner and consider the probable effect upon the shares in your existing portfolio and any future selections you might have under review. When you first heard about video recorders, you would almost certainly have concluded that they would prove to be a worldwide success. Your difficulty would have been to select a particular company that would benefit. Most major electrical manufacturers produced their own video recorders so the benefits were spread thinly throughout the industry. This is frequently the case unless a product can be patented — a vital factor that you should always bear in mind.

Unlike new management and a patented product, some new developments, such as the collapse of a major competitor, only have a short-term effect. Obviously, there is an on-going benefit, but the major impact comes during the first year, and the acceleration in earnings in that year may not be repeatable.

A new acquisition can often have a major impact upon a company's earnings and status. When Hanson took over Imperial Tobacco, the company instantly became a major part of the fabric of British industry, with enormous cash flow and financial strength. Of course, Hanson was a great company before the acquisition, but afterwards it was regarded in a different light.

I give below a few examples of something new from each of the four categories with graphs showing how the shares reacted subsequently:

1. NEW MANAGEMENT

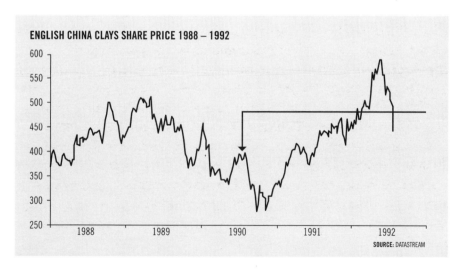

ANDREW TEARE

(i) ENGLISH CHINA CLAYS - Andrew Teare's appointment as Chief Executive of the company in the summer of 1990 has had far-reaching results for the group. He has since disposed of non-core assets totalling £110m to concentrate upon the core activities and made a £310m acquisition of a china clays business in the U.S.A.. By June 1992, the share price had doubled from its Autumn 1990 low.

MIKE HENNESSY

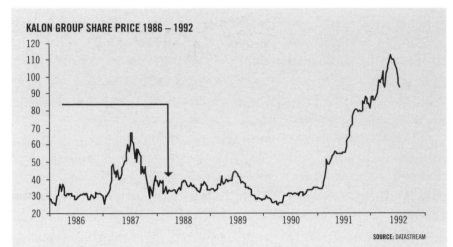

(ii) KALON GROUP - Since Mike Hennessy from Dixons moved in as Managing Director in February 1988, losses have been eliminated and £17m of debt has been repaid. 1988 profits and earnings per share have increased nearly 150% despite the recession, and net cash stood at £12.8m at the end of the last financial year.

RON GARRICK

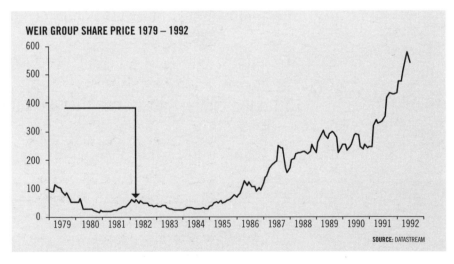

(iii) WEIR GROUP - During the early 1980s, Weir was losing £10m per annum and looked like becoming a victim of that recession. Since Ron Garrick's appointment as Managing Director in 1982, the group has been slimmed down to two core divisions and the workforce has been slashed. Profits have grown steadily in recent years, exceeding £30m in 1991. The dividend has trebled during the last five years.

2. NEW PRODUCTS OR TECHNOLOGY

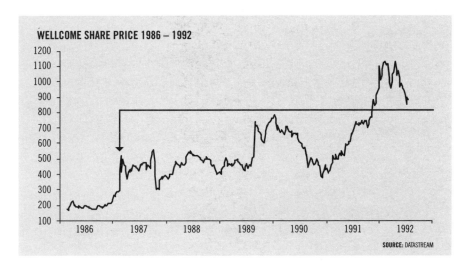

WELLCOME SHARE PRICE 1986 – 1992

SOURCE: DATASTREAM

(i) WELLCOME - The development of Retrovir for the treatment of AIDS helped the company's profits to soar after the product was launched in March 1987. The drug enjoys high margins and is forecast to keep expanding sales for many years to come.

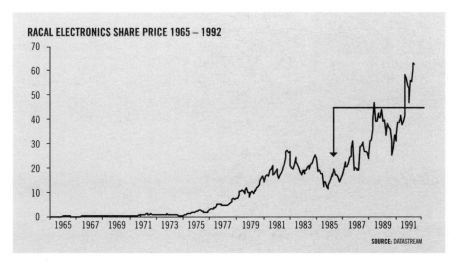

RACAL ELECTRONICS SHARE PRICE 1965 – 1992

SOURCE: DATASTREAM

(ii) RACAL ELECTRONICS - The extraordinary success of the Vodafone business, launched in 1985, has done wonders for Racal's share price. Vodafone was floated off as a separate company in September 1991, valued at £3.5bn.

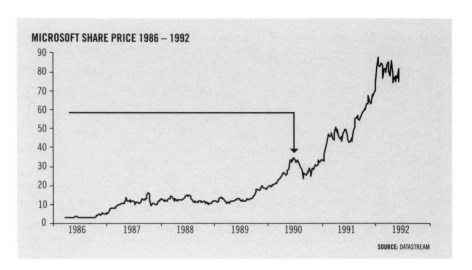

(iii) MICROSOFT - An American NASDAQ company which revolutionised the computer industry with its highly popular 'Windows 3' software in June 1990. Two years later Microsoft was capitalised at $20bn.

3.   NEW EVENTS IN THE INDUSTRY AS A WHOLE

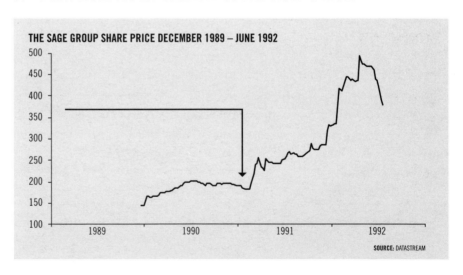

(i)   SAGE GROUP - The financial difficulties of Pegasus, its main competitor in the UK, helped Sage to secure 74% of the accounting software market for small companies and 43% of the total small business software market.

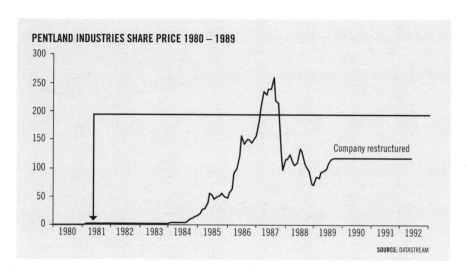

(ii) PENTLAND GROUP - Bought in 1981 for a mere $77,500, a substantial stake in Reebok became worth more than $700m on the back of a swing towards sports shoes as fashion accessories and the craze among American women for Reebok's specially designed aerobics shoes. As the investment in Reebok soon became Pentland's main asset, this new consumer trend had a massive impact on Pentland's share price.

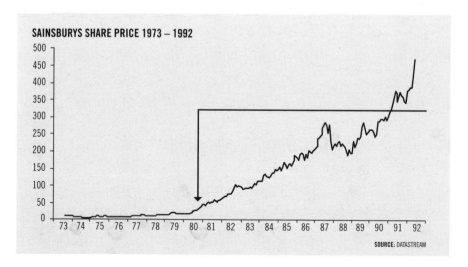

(iii) SAINSBURY - In the early eighties, the acceleration of the trend towards out of town shopping and hypermarkets enabled companies like Sainsbury and Tesco to grab more market share from smaller players, and has helped to fuel their rapid growth. Another by-product has been improved margins.

4. NEW ACQUISITIONS

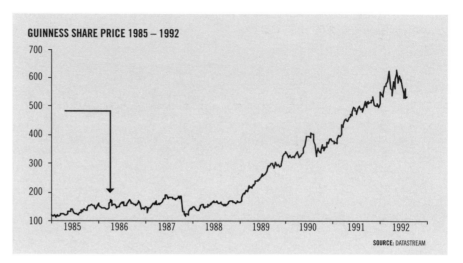

(i) GUINNESS - The controversial acquisition of Distillers for £2.7bn in 1986 strengthened Guinness's brand portfolio making it one of the finest in the world. In June 1992, the company was capitalised at over £12bn compared with less than £1bn before the bid, and the shares had appreciated by 300%.

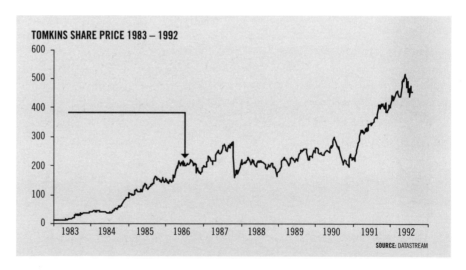

(ii) TOMKINS - The successful £192m hostile bid for Pegler-Hattersley in the summer of 1986 transformed Tomkins into a major league predator. In the year to May 1987, Tomkins' pre-tax profits quadrupled to £30.1m, sales rose from £63M to £270m and earnings per share jumped 70%. By September 1987, the company was capitalised at £360m, and was primed for a succession of further bids on its way to a market capitalisation of £1.4bn and a place in the FT-SE 100 Index.

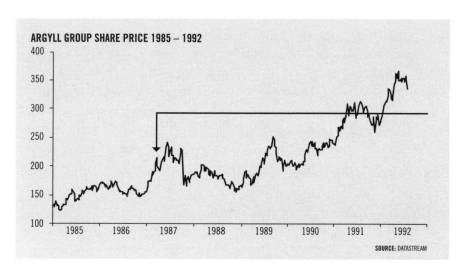

ARGYLL GROUP SHARE PRICE 1985 – 1992

SOURCE: DATASTREAM

(iii) ARGYLL GROUP - After failing in its bid for Distillers, Argyll focused on food retailing. The acquisition of Safeway for £680m, in February 1987, enabled the company to take a quantum leap into the supermarket top echelon. Argyll's market capitalisation has increased from £700m before its first bid for Distillers to £3.9bn in June 1992, while sales have more than doubled to £5bn and pre-tax profits have nearly quintupled. The share price is up 75% since the purchase, despite the 1987 crash and a jittery period for the shares in 1988.

There is an added advantage of identifying something new. The story of the stock becomes much more interesting and easy to relate to, resulting in quicker acceptance by the market. The less fundamental support for a share price, the more necessary it is for there to be a good story to give the hope of increased future earnings. If current earnings do not support the share price, hopes of future earnings growth are sometimes all that the share has going for it.

In June 1992, the story of Bernard Taylor and Medeva, for example, could have been passed from broker to private client in this way:

'Bernard Taylor was Chief Executive of Glaxo. He joined a very small company, Medeva, a couple of years ago. Since then it has made a number of brilliant acquisitions — drug selling organisations in the States, generic drug manufacturers and now it is the biggest supplier of vaccines. It is quite likely to make a big take-over soon. On Medeva's multiple, anything it buys will enhance assets and earnings per share. The shares could go a lot higher — Medeva is another Glaxo in the making.'

BERNARD TAYLOR

You have to admit that the story is terrific. A large number of people do appear to believe in Medeva, and as a result, in June 1992, the company was capitalised at about £525m on an historic multiple of over 30. Call me old fashioned, but if I was buying into a healthcare business, I would prefer a more established and debt-free company like Amersham International, growing at over 25% per annum on an historic multiple of 20. Medeva has to produce a very substantial increase in earnings to be level with this quality company. Avoid astronomic multiples — companies like Medeva may succeed, but if they falter for a moment there is no safety factor and the share price would collapse.

In telling you about Medeva, I have side-tracked a little from my main point, which I will repeat — the added advantage of something new is that the story of the stock is easy to explain, and the market will quickly grasp it. A good story is a powerful catalyst to help the share price on its upward path. The market likes a good story, and something new adds both piquancy and interest.

The story is also important as a cross-check for you. If you buy a share with passable fundamentals and a good story, you must constantly check that the status quo is unchanged. The story invariably boils down to the reasons for hoping that there will be a substantial increase in future earnings. You must continually refer back to the original story and check each new development against it. Make a quick exit if there are material changes for the worse.

As you read on you will be amazed by the number of the criteria for my system which inter-relate with each other. The hip bone is connected to the thigh bone, the thigh bone is connected to the knee bone and so on. Something new is often the cause of relative strength of the shares in the market, of an acceleration in earnings and of an improvement in the estimates of future growth rates and therefore of the PEG factor. Sometimes, when I take a closer look at a share, I discover that something new happened a year or so ago that caused the fundamentals to change. For example, in 1991, I liked Whessoe shares because the prospective multiple was only 7, the earnings growth rate was approximately 15% per annum, the company had a strong liquid position and seemed to be moving from heavy industry to the more attractive instruments business. Whessoe had just purchased an Italian competitor of MTL Instruments. When I examined the position in more detail, I found that a couple of years earlier a new Managing Director and Finance Director had been appointed. Here was the something new that had caused the change in earnings, future growth prospects and the perception of the company as a whole.

As the essential criteria of my system do inter-relate so much, look for one criterion to confirm another. If earnings are accelerating and/or the share price has good relative strength, expect there to be an explanation.

LET ME SUMMARISE FOR YOU THE MAIN POINTS MADE IN THIS CHAPTER:

1. Something new is highly desirable but not absolutely mandatory, especially when the company fulfills most of my other criteria.

2. The main categories of something new are new management, products or technology, a new acquisition or a new event in the industry as a whole, including legislation.

3. New management is the best of these because the effects can be so far-reaching and are on-going.

4. New products, events and acquisitions have to be of sufficient importance to the company in question to increase future earnings substantially.

5. A distinction has to be made between gimmicky one-off products and others that are likely to be long-lasting.

6. The effect of new events like the collapse of a competitor in an industry can be limited to one or two years' earnings. New legislation can be much longer lasting.

7. An added advantage of something new is that it provides a ready-made story for the stock, which helps the shares to gain market acceptance and can be used as a way of monitoring future developments. A good story is most important when present fundamentals are poor, as future hopes aided by the story will be the fuel to drive the share price upwards.

8. As you read about a major new development, product or event make a conscious effort to think of the likely effect upon the shares in your existing portfolio and upon any future selections.

9. Something new is often a superb confirmation that my other criteria are satisfied. For example, something new will frequently be the cause of accelerating earnings, a higher prospective growth rate, a lower PEG and high relative strength of the shares in the market. Frequently something new is the missing piece of the jigsaw.

7
—

COMPETITIVE ADVANTAGE

COMPETITIVE ADVANTAGE IS A CRUCIALLY IMPORTANT FURTHER CRITERION WHICH YOU MUST FULLY UNDERSTAND.

Imagine that you have identified a dreamlike company, which appears to be growing at 20% per annum, with a P/E ratio of only 10 and a very attractive PEG factor of only 0.5. When you find a share growing at this rate, you know, almost for certain, that at some point in the future, the P/E ratio will be at least 20 and the share would then have a PEG factor of one. However, in a particularly heady phase of the stockmarket, the multiple could easily rise as high as 25 to 30 times earnings. It is important to understand that the P/E ratio will certainly rise as more and more investors realise that the company churns out earnings increasing at a steady rate of 20% per annum. Going forward five years, earnings would increase from say 10p a share to 25p, and if by then the multiple had risen to 20, the share price would be 500p. This compares with 100p originally, when the dream share was on a multiple of only 10. A gain of 400% — a licence to print money, provided that earnings continued to grow at 20% per annum. You might argue that four or five years could elapse before the multiple rose to 20 or more, but you know that it would simply be a matter of time — not a case of if, but when.

Let us go back to the important proviso, that earnings must grow at

20% per annum. This assumption would have to be based upon as much supporting evidence as possible. I know that you would check the consensus of brokers' estimates, the outlook for the industry, the past record of the company and the Chairman's forecast, but there is also another vital criterion that you should apply. You should seek to establish the company's competitive advantage, which will underpin your earnings growth projections and give them the *reliability* you are seeking.

Edge is another word for competitive advantage. Something extra, hard to beat and difficult to emulate. If you were living in a small town, which of these businesses would you prefer to own?:

1. The only local newspaper, established for thirty years.
2. A local gravel pit with the only supply of gravel within a forty mile radius.
3. An engineering business that supplies parts and accessories to a leading motor manufacturer and other UK customers of a similar nature.
4. A local builder and decorator, established for fifty years with no major competitors.

My question is of course heavily loaded. Other people would be unlikely to try to set up in opposition to the local newspaper. Most of the townsfolk would only want to read one local newspaper a week, and there would be insufficient demand in the town to support two of them. The gravel business is again almost impossible to compete with. Planning permission would be required for another gravel pit, and most local councils would not want another eyesore on their doorstep. Also, the cost of transport is such a high proportion of the selling price of gravel that competition from much further away would be out of the question.

The engineering business is very different. The motor manufacturer would have definite views on the prices to be paid for his supplies. The owner of the business would do his best to negotiate but the customer would have the final say, and as the products of the business would not be branded or special in any way, the motor manufacturer could always find another supplier. You can see the contrast with the newspaper proprietor, who could increase advertising prices much more easily. So could the gravel supplier, as long as he kept his prices at a level that still made supply from another area an uneconomic proposition.

The building and decorating business is hardly worth a second thought. There might be no serious competition for years, but the threat would always be there. Very little equipment would be needed for a local handyman who had just retired from other employment to set up as a decorator. He could undercut our building and decorating firm, do a good job, be quickly recommended to other customers and, before you could wink, a friend might join him and they would have an instant decorating business.

In this small town it is easy to see that the first two businesses have a competitive advantage over the others. A clear edge. Now, I want to show you how to identify the competitive advantage of quoted companies on both a national and international scale.

A company has a considerable advantage over competitors through owning one or more great brand names. Coca Cola comes immediately to mind as one of the best-known products in the world. Other examples are Nestlé and Sony. All three companies have supplied quality products over the years and have reinforced their quality image in the public's mind through persistent and massive advertising. In the UK, Cadbury Schweppes, Guinness and Marks & Spencer are obvious candidates. Their brand names are in themselves tremendous assets that make them very difficult to compete with.

Given the choice, you would rather invest in a business that has a distinct advantage over other businesses than one which is at an obvious disadvantage and open to attack from all and sundry. Not unnaturally, you would prefer the invulnerable to the vulnerable. Businesses like Cadbury Schweppes, Guinness and Marks & Spencer have strong business franchises in the sense that they are comparatively invulnerable and almost impossible to compete with. In contrast, businesses that do not have a franchise of any kind, like small restaurants, dress shops, builders and decorators and general engineering businesses, are very vulnerable. Almost anyone could set up in opposition with a small capital outlay and very little difficulty. Their failure rate is therefore high, as margins frequently come under extreme pressure.

Warren Buffett, the legendary American investor, looks for companies that have good business franchises. Coca Cola, Gillette and Disney would all qualify. In 1991, Buffett invested in Guinness. He sums up this important facet of his philosophy in his own inimitable manner:

'The test of a franchise is what a smart guy with a lot of money could do to it if he tried. If you gave me a billion dollars, and you gave me first draft pick of fifty business managers throughout the United States, I could cream both the business world and the journalistic world. If you said 'Go take the *Wall Street Journal*', I would hand you back the billion dollars.

Now, incidentally, if you gave me a similar amount of money and you told me to make a dent in the profitability of or change the market position of the Omaha National Bank or the leading department store in Omaha, I could give them a very hard time. I might not do much for you in the process, but I could cause them a lot of trouble. The real test of a business is how much damage a competitor can do, even if he is stupid about returns.

There are some businesses that have very large moats around them with crocodiles, sharks and piranhas in. Those are the sorts of businesses you want. You want some business that, going back to my day, Johnny Weissmuller in a suit of armour could not make across the moat. There are businesses like that.'

WARREN BUFFETT

I like Warren Buffett's homespun style. I can see exactly what he means, although I think he mixes his metaphors a little. The suit of armour might keep out the crocodiles, sharks and piranhas, but even Hollywood's Tarzan of the Apes would have found chain mail too much of a handicap when swimming a moat.

A similar competitive advantage exists with products that are patented. I have already mentioned Wellcome, which patented Retrovir, their medicant for the treatment of A.I.D.S., and made a fortune by doing so. Patents normally last for sixteen years, but by the time they expire the brand name and acceptance of the product are often so strong that competitors can only make a small dent in profitability.

RICHARD BRANSON

Copyrights last fifty years and can be extraordinarily valuable. The sale of Richard Branson's Virgin Records to Thorn EMI for £550m illustrates the value of copyright records. Film libraries are also becoming increasingly valuable with the worldwide growth of cable and satellite television, coupled with the inflated cost of making comparable films today. A large number of new broadcasters are now desperately seeking more product.

Government legislation sometimes creates monopolies and oligopolies by granting business franchises. Utilities and cable TV companies are among the best known examples. There is a snag with these kinds of businesses however — they are usually closely regulated so that the customer cannot be abused by unsubstantiated price increases.

Warren Buffett has something to say on this subject too:

'If I had the only water company in Omaha, I would do fine if I didn't have a regulator. What you are looking for is an unregulated water company.'

A less precise area is the position some companies achieve by simply being by far the biggest and most dominant in their industry. Potential competitors find the idea of entering the industry too daunting a prospect. Good examples in this country are the *Financial Times* and Rentokil. You will readily appreciate that the advantage of scale is less attractive to a potential investor than a 'business franchise' with very strong brand names, patented or copyright products or protection by government legislation. For leading companies the risk of competition is undoubtedly greater today as business is so international. General Motors and BMC found this to their cost when the Japanese began to concentrate upon the motor industry. IBM too has been feeling the draught since the early seventies.

A different kind of edge over competitors can be obtained by having a niche business with a substantial market share. For example, Druck is a world leader in pressure measuring devices. This kind of business always runs the slight risk that a major company may decide to enter its industry, but for them to do so successfully would probably take more money and effort than would be justified. The risk grows as their markets become bigger and more worthwhile, but meanwhile they usually continue to earn excellent margins and grow far better and more reliably than the average company.

It is instructive to study the performance of different sectors of the stockmarket over the last twelve years. You will see overleaf how industries which enjoyed the benefit of patents and strong brand names massively outperformed those with no business franchise.

I am not in the least surprised that the Health and Household sector of the market has shown the best return to investors. The businesses in this sector often have patented products with international appeal. High on the list too are brewers, food manufacturers and food retailers, who are protected and helped by their strong brand names. Near the bottom, as expected, you find engineering companies, especially the metal bashers with no branded products or business franchises of any kind. New competitors can easily enter their field. Similarly the dull performance of textile companies is no surprise to me.

PERCENTAGE PERFORMANCE OF SELECTED FTA SECTOR INDICES 1980 – 1992

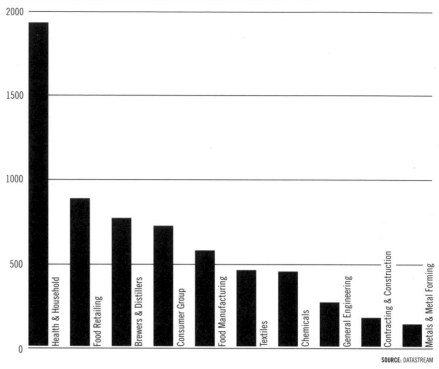

SOURCE: DATASTREAM

These figures may lead you to wonder why any money is ever invested in conventional general engineering companies and in companies with unbranded products in the textile industry. There is, of course, a price for everything but I share your puzzlement. I am also surprised that anyone invests in companies with earnings in decline, companies that have an unattractive P/E ratio, companies that are borrowing far too much and companies that have rapidly declining profit margins. I have long ago stopped worrying about these anomolies though, and thank God there are still some people who do invest in these companies. The important thing to remember is not to join them. You do not have to follow their example. You are looking for companies that have something extra — a competitive advantage. Also, the shares you will be choosing have to satisfy a number of highly selective additional criteria. Not many companies will make the grade.

The brand names of companies like Coca Cola and Guinness are self-evident and very well-known. You know their products and know that the companies in question have a substantial competitive advantage. Your knowledge will be an important factor when you come to the chapter on selecting leading shares and American shares.

A CROSS SECTION OF PRE-TAX PROFIT MARGINS 1987 – 1991

EXCELLENT

Year	Turnover £bn	Pre-tax Profit £bn	Pre-tax Margin %
GLAXO			
1987	1.74	0.75	43.1
1988	2.06	0.83	40.3
1989	2.57	1.01	39.3
1990	3.18	1.18	37.1
1991	3.40	1.28	37.6

GOOD

Year	Turnover £m	Pre-tax Profit £m	Pre-tax Margin %
MTL			
1987	7.5	1.79	23.9
1988	9.3	2.31	24.8
1989	11.9	3.08	25.9
1990	14.0	3.77	26.9
1991	18.0	4.61	25.6
RENTOKIL			
1987	174	37.6	21.6
1988	213	50.1	23.5
1989	279	62.0	22.2
1990	309	74.7	24.2
1991	389	94.6	24.3
SPRING RAM			
1987	61	10.7	17.5
1988	85	16.6	19.5
1989	121	24.1	19.9
1990	145	30.1	20.8
1991	194	37.6	19.4

FAIR

Year	Turnover £m	Pre-tax Profit £m	Pre-tax Margin %
VICTAULIC			
1987	51.8	6.5	12.5
1988	62.9	7.6	12.1
1989	78.3	8.8	11.2
1990	99.6	11.5	11.5
1991	115.0	14.3	12.4
RANK HOVIS MCDOUGALL			
1987	1,540	118	7.7
1988	1,670	157	9.4
1989	1,790	176	9.8
1990	1,770	131	7.4
1991	1,530	150	9.8

POOR

Year	Turnover £m	Pre-tax Profit £m	Pre-tax Margin %
DALGETY			
1987	5,000	93	1.9
1988	4,500	100	2.2
1989	4,760	110	2.3
1990	4,630	118	2.5
1991	3,770	111	2.9
BRIDON			
1987	196	7.7	3.9
1988	213	13.5	6.3
1989	305	16.0	5.2
1990	336	10.1	3.0
1991	319	-3.6	-1.1
BRITISH AEROSPACE			
1987	4,100	-159	-3.9
1988	5,600	236	4.2
1989	9,100	333	3.7
1990	10,500	376	3.6
1991	10,600	-81	-0.8

Smaller companies are more likely to own lesser-known brand names, patents and copyrights that will eventually become very well-known if they continue to be successful. They are more likely to be in a dominant or very strong position in a niche business. Recognising these characteristics is very difficult. The first step is to narrow down the field. We know that, with very few exceptions, we are not interested in textiles, heavy plant and machinery, general engineering and electrical businesses, building and contracting, the automotive industry and banks. You will notice that I have used the word 'general' when eliminating engineering and electrical businesses, whereas the other industries like textiles have been swept away without qualification. The reason is simple - there are a large number of niche businesses with excellent products in the engineering and electrical section of the market. Common sense will tell you that both MTL and Druck are on to a good thing. There is, however, another useful rule-of-thumb to aid you in your research — if a well managed company is established in a growing niche business, profit margins will be healthily positive and will be tending to increase. Beware if they are declining rapidly. With a company operating on profit margins of only 5% there is little room for error. With the exception of food retailing, for the reasons explained in Chapter Five, 7.5% is a minimum starting base, and 10% to 20% is more in line with our requirements. Companies always state their turnover, so profit margins are easy to calculate. Look at the examples on the previous page.

Some allowance does of course have to be made for general trading conditions. But not much — the best companies will survive recessions better than most and some of the stronger niche businesses will hardly notice them. Glaxo, MTL, Rentokil and Spring Ram have all been excellent investments, massively outperforming companies with no business franchise like Dalgety and Bridon.

Companies with strong business franchises usually enjoy an excellent return on capital employed. Industrial businesses tend to yield far less on capital than 'people' businesses such as advertising agencies and insurance brokers, which can show extraordinarily high returns, if goodwill is not factored into the equation. With a small industrial business, I like to see a return of between 20% and 25%. Not so high that it will attract excessive competition but high enough to generate plenty of future growth. The percentage is calculated as follows:

1. Capital employed is the sum of ordinary share capital, preference shares, debentures, loan stocks and other debt.

2. Average the capital employed at the beginning and end of the financial year.
3. Add back interest payable and preference dividends to the profits before tax.
4. Express 3. as a percentage of 2.

Let us take the example of Kalon in 1991. By examining the group balance sheet you can see that shareholders' funds (or the net assets) were £28.002m in 1991 and £24.463m in 1990. The other items that must be added to these figures are short-term debts, amounts due under finance leases and hire purchase agreements, long-term debt and

KALON GROUP BALANCE SHEET

31st December 1991	Note	1991 £000	1990 £000
Fixed Assets			
Tangible assets	10	20,256	19,887
Investments	11	46	500
		20,302	20,387
Current Assets			
Stocks	13	13,255	13,094
Debtors	14	16,899	14,664
Cash at bank and in hand		14,607	3,643
		44,761	31,401
Creditors due within one year			
Bank overdraft and loans		610	243
Trade creditors		13,386	14,091
Other creditors	15	20,727	11,285
		34,723	25,619
Net current assets		10,038	5,782
Total assets less current liabilities		30,340	26,169
Creditors due after more than one year	16	(648)	(589)
Provisions for liabilities and charges	17	(1,690)	(1,117)
		28,002	24,463
Capital and reserves			
Called up share capital	20	17,930	17,824
Reserves			
Share premium account	21	296	205
Revaluation reserve	21	4,860	4,860
Profit and loss account	21	4,916	1,574
Shareholders' funds		28,002	24,463

KALON NOTES TO THE ACCOUNTS

	1991		1990	
Note 15 *Other Creditors*	*Group* *£000*	*Company* *£000*	*Group* *£000*	*Company* *£000*
Finance leases and hire purchase agreements	572	572	437	437
Corporation tax	3,834	3,822	2,515	2,515
Other taxes and social security	3,089	3,004	1,988	1,977
Other creditors	552	332	533	263
Accruals	10,887	10,673	4,624	4,507
Dividend	1,793	1,793	1,188	1,188
	20,727	20,196	11,285	10,887

Note 16 *Creditors due after more than 1 year*				
Finance leases and hire purchase agreements due within 2 to 5 years	323	323	264	264
8.25% loan repayable in equal instalments:				
Between 2 to 5 years	81	81	81	81
In more than 5 years	244	244	244	244
	648	648	589	589

Note 17 *Provision for liabilities and charges*				
Deferred taxation (see note 19)	-	-	160	160
Pension equalisation	1,690	1,690	957	957
	1,690	1,690	1,117	1,117

provisions. The only short-term debt that needs to be included is 'Bank overdraft and loans' shown under the general heading of 'Creditors due within one year'. In Note 15 'Other creditors', you find the amount due for finance leases and HP agreements. In Notes 16 and 17 you find long-term debts and provisions.

The capital side of the equation is therefore calculated like this:

	1991 (£000)	1990 (£000)
Net assets	28002	24463
Short-term debt	610	243
Leases, HP	572	437
Long-term debt	648	589
Provisions	1690	1117
	31522	26849

The average for the year, obtained by simply adding the two totals together and dividing by two, is usually a more accurate measure as capital employed can fluctuate throughout the period. In this case it amounts to £29.186m.

The other half of the equation is the pre-tax profit figure after adding back interest payable and preference dividends. In Kalon's case this is shown as Operating Profit of £9.177m. To obtain the return on average capital employed, expressed as a percentage, you make the following calculation:

$$\frac{9{,}177{,}000}{29{,}186{,}000} \quad x \quad 100 \quad = \quad 31.4\%$$

The future growth of a company's earnings stems to a large extent from the profits, less tax and dividends, ploughed back into the business. *The capacity to employ capital at a high rate of return is one of the surest marks of a true growth stock.* For example, Rentokil enjoys a five year average rate of return of 53%, and Glaxo is also well above the norm at 37%.

You will notice that I have just mentioned a five year average for Rentokil and Glaxo. This is a far more reliable way of judging the capacity of a business to employ capital exceptionally well. The trend can be important, and the five year average tends to iron out accounting quirks. Now for the good news — if your brokers have access to Datastream, they should be able to obtain all the details for you.

Another interesting way of looking at a share that produces a high rate of return on capital on a regular and reliable basis is to compare it with a gilt. If a gilt produced a return of 20% per annum, of course it would command a premium price of well over par. There is little point in investing in shares which have a low rate of return on capital employed, if you can find companies that have a superior competitive advantage.

A good example of a small company that has an excellent business franchise is Glass's Guide, now owned by International Thomson Organisation. As the definitive monthly guide for second-hand car dealers, its product is not unduly price-sensitive. It would be difficult for a competitor to set up in opposition. You should be on the alert to identify other businesses of this kind, and intent on avoiding companies with main products which have an obvious risk of substitution. Whoever used to manufacture gas lamps would, I am sure, endorse this caveat. Also beware of companies that are very dependent upon one customer or one supplier, as margins could easily come under extreme

pressure. Companies with a product or service that is generally available are always vulnerable to price wars, which can have a devastating effect on margins. For example, in America there was cut-throat competition when the airlines were de-regulated, and such well-known companies as TWA and Pan-Am were forced into Chapter Eleven — the brink of bankruptcy.

I find it particularly pleasing that each facet of my system inter-relates so well with other facets. Once you have identified a business with a competitive advantage — a strong business franchise — you will usually find that the earnings record is excellent, the growth prospects are good, easy to predict and *reliable*, and that the share has high relative strength in the stock market. One criterion reinforces another. All of them taken together help to ensure that your final selection is a strong one.

A NUMBER OF IMPORTANT POINTS HAVE BEEN MADE IN THIS CHAPTER :

1.   The competitive advantage of a company underpins future earnings estimates and increases the *reliability* of profit forecasts.

2.   Competitive advantage, sometimes called 'business franchise', arises in several different ways:
     i.   Excellent brand names
     ii.   Patents or copyrights
     iii.   Government legislation creating franchises (although usually with some regulation)
     iv.   An established position in a niche market
     v.   Dominance in an industry
     This list is broadly in order of invulnerability to competition.

3.   Leading companies are more likely to possess excellent brand names, patents and copyrights. Smaller companies will tend to have products with this kind of *potential* and/or an established position in a niche business.

4.   Avoid companies that are too dependent upon one main supplier or customer, and companies in an industry which is well-known for the intense rivalry between competitors. Also beware of products that might easily be substituted.

5. Dislike companies in the *general* engineering and electrical business, textiles, building and contracting and the motor industry. Prefer businesses in health and household products, food retailing and manufacture and brewers and distillers.

6. A cross-check on competitive advantage, especially in niche businesses, is through profit margins. Expressed as a percentage of turnover, these should be at least 7.5% and preferably 10% to 20%. Avoid companies with very low profit margins and look especially for increasing profit margins.

7. *The most reliable evidence of a company with a strong competitive advantage is the ability of the management to employ capital at a well above average rate of return.* Over 20% per annum is your target for industrial companies. Your broker should be able to obtain five year figures from Datastream.

8. When my system of stockmarket investment works at its best, all the criteria inter-relate. If you have identified a company with a strong business franchise, the return on capital employed is likely to be above average, the earnings record first class, the growth prospects reliable and the shares should have high relative strength in the stockmarket.

To find a company with a business franchise is not too difficult, but if you are one of the last people to see the potential the multiple will already be astronomic. We are seeking perfection — a strong business franchise at a reasonable price.

8

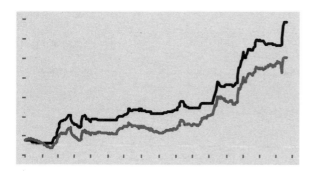

MOMENTUM AND RELATIVE STRENGTH

ABOUT TWENTY YEARS AGO, I OBSERVED THAT CHARTISTS USUALLY HAD DIRTY RAINCOATS AND LARGE OVERDRAFTS. At the time I was thinking of an acquaintance who had fared very badly using technical analysis. Even now I do not know many rich chartists. However, since those early days, I have met one or two who have made their fortune and read about a few more, so I give technical analysis much more credence than before.

In essence, chartists believe that a chart showing the history of a share price reflects the hopes and fears of all investors and is essentially based upon the one indisputable fact — how the share price has actually performed in the market-place. A technical analyst would argue that the market's perception of a share is a constantly changing illusion. For example, Glaxo's multiple has fluctuated between 13.4 and 33.8 during the years 1985 to 1992. Glaxo has remained a growth share throughout that period, but the stockmarket's perception of the value of a Glaxo share has been continually changing.

Chartists also argue that when share prices move up and down they are likely to trend, and that it is more important to follow the trend than to try to work out the likely earnings per share several years ahead. When an experienced chartist examines a share, he or she will be able to suggest the best point of entry for making a purchase — a point on the chart, where the downside risk is minimised and the upside potential is maximised.

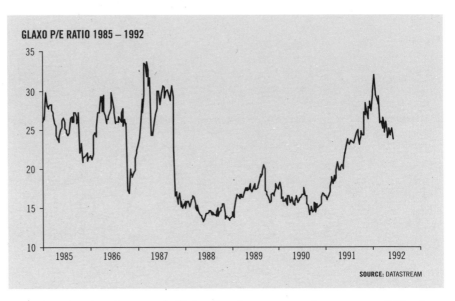

GLAXO P/E RATIO 1985 – 1992

SOURCE: DATASTREAM

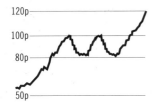

Trends often become self-feeding for reasons that are not difficult to understand. Imagine a share that has risen from 50p to 100p and then falls back to 80p, only to rise again to 100p, fall back again to 80p and then go straight to 120p.

During the consolidation period, when the price ranged from 80p to 100p, many willing sellers would eventually lower their selling limits to achieve a sale. This would of course thin out supply. Similarly, many buyers at under 80p would eventually raise their limits to buy within the trading range, helping to further exhaust the supply and increase the share price. As the price breaks upwards, many investors will let profits run and many fresh buyers will raise their limits to acquire the stock. There is nothing quite like the feeling of greed that comes over you when a share you really fancy seems to be escaping your clutches. You reach for it, pay more and the upward trend becomes self-reinforcing.

I prefer to look upon charts as a tool in the kit, not an end in themselves. Charts provide me with further confirmation that I am proceeding along the right lines, or, alternatively, give me a warning signal, sometimes well in advance of any apparent deterioration in the fundamentals.

When you invest in dynamic growth companies that have strong fundamentals and are due for a status change, the shares should be performing better than the average of the market as a whole. Your broker, almost certainly, subscribes to Datastream and should be able to supply you with charts showing the relative strength of your selections against the FT-A All-Share Index.

Here are four charts showing the relative strength of MTL, Sage, Rentokil and GEC from early 1991 to June 1992.

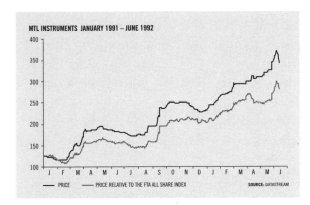

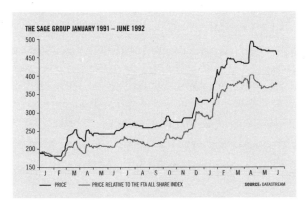

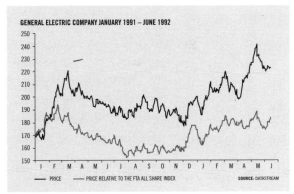

As you can see, there is no argument about the excellent performance of MTL and Sage, both of which have left the market far behind. Rentokil has also performed well, but has not had the benefit of a major status change in its multiple which has always been on the high side. GEC has been a dull dog, and its relative performance against the market has been poor.

Some brokers provide their institutional clients on a regular basis with details of the relative price action of a large number of shares in major companies. There are also chart services to which you can subscribe, but for practical purposes the Datastream charts give an instant picture of how most shares have been performing relative to the market.

Another rule-of-thumb is to invest in this kind of growth share only when the price is within 15% of its high. This may sound paradoxical as obviously you would prefer to buy a share at a lower price rather than a higher one. However, if a growth share is more than 15% below its high there could be something wrong with the fundamentals — some news that you have not yet heard that is being signalled to you by the poor price action of the shares.

Further evidence of the importance of relative strength is provided by William O'Neil in his book *How to Make Money in Stocks*. He made a study of the 500 best-performing listed US equities from 1953 to 1990 and found that these stocks averaged an extraordinarily high relative strength rating of 87, during the period before their major price increase began. In other words, on average the 500 stocks out-performed 87% of other stocks in the comparison group during the critical period prior to purchase.

When investing in asset situations, you are not looking for relative strength in the shares. With asset situations you long for the shares to be neglected while you accumulate them, and you might even buy more if they fall a little. You should *never* average down when buying a growth share.

I am not an expert on charts but I am a friend of Brian Marber, who is one of the leading chartists in the UK, so I decided to ask him for his recommendations on buying and selling signals on individual shares. In Chapter Eighteen, I also question him on the market as a whole.

When Brian Marber was at Simon and Coates, in his circulars on Technical Analysis he included some *'Great Lies of the City'*. They are still pertinent today:

'All the loose stock is now in firm hands.'

'I know that I can rely on you to keep this to yourself.'

'Yours is the only research that doesn't go into the waste paper basket.'

'I am feeling completely relaxed about the situation.'

'We are essentially long-term investors and are therefore not interested in short-term market fluctuations.'

Brian is Chairman of Brian Marber and Co., consultants on foreign exchange and stockmarkets using technical analysis.

Here are the verbatim details of my interview with him:

JS *I have explained that Datastream charts and my 15% rule are methods of checking the relative strength of a share. Do you agree with these?*

BM Absolutely. I had not heard of the 15% rule, but it certainly makes a lot of sense to me.

JS *Are there any other ways that would be easy and practical for the average investor?*

BM I like to see shares break out of a base area but, very often, growth shares do not form base areas at all, and they can only be found by using a relative strength chart.

JS *How do you read a chart for relative strength? What are the good and bad signs?*

BM I read the chart of relative strength just as I would the chart of any other share. I look at patterns, moving averages, trendlines and momentum. A sequence of higher highs and lows is obviously a good sign, whereas a bad sign would be a sequence of lower highs and lows.

BREAK OUT FROM A BASE AREA – KWIK FIT

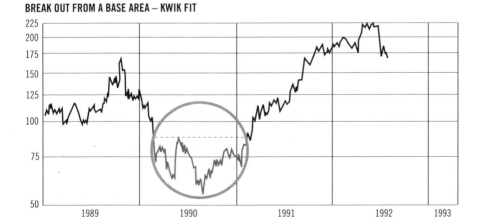

SOURCE: INVESTMENT RESEARCH OF CAMBRIDGE LTD.

JS   *I always like a growth share that has had a reasonably long period of price consolidation and appears to be about to break out into new high ground. Does this particular pattern have a special name and do you have any pointers to help find this kind of share?*

BM   As I said, very frequently a growth share won't have a long period of price consolidation, although its relative strength chart might have a pattern like that.

JS   *How do you tell if a share with excellent relative strength is about to fall or that there is any likelihood that it will do so?*

BM   I think it is always difficult to sell a share that has excellent relative strength, but it is of course possible that while the relative strength curve is rising, the chart of the share itself is forming a top area — a head and shoulders, double top or descending triangle. But in each of these cases it would be impossible to sell at the top of the market. Anyway, much as technical analysts like to sell at the top and buy at the bottom, technical analysis being essentially a trend-following discipline, is unlikely to pick absolute highs or lows. Indeed, since I believe that technical analysts are not meant to anticipate the market — the technical analyst is quite likely to be caught at tops and bottoms because he is extrapolating the trend.

DOUBLE TOP – C. E. HEATH

SOURCE: INVESTMENT RESEARCH OF CAMBRIDGE LTD.

JS   *I understand that when a share price falls below its 90 or 180 day moving average, that is a signal of probable future weakness. Is that so?*

HEAD AND SHOULDERS (TOP) – ARGOS

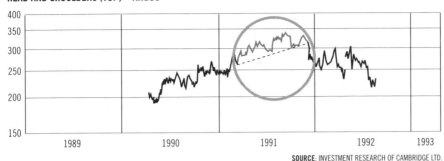

SOURCE: INVESTMENT RESEARCH OF CAMBRIDGE LTD.

HEAD AND SHOULDERS (REVERSAL) – INCHCAPE

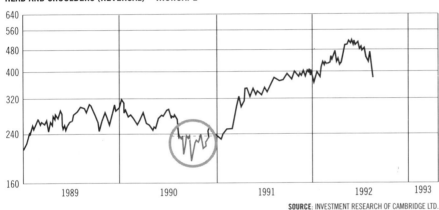

SOURCE: INVESTMENT RESEARCH OF CAMBRIDGE LTD.

BM   Not necessarily. Actually, I use 63 and 253 day averages (three
trading months and a trading year) and have often found that
intermediate reactions frequently end very soon after a share has
pulled back to or beneath its 63 day average. You can't tell
whether any particular contact with the 63 or the 90 day
average is going to produce a rally and can only discipline
yourself like this - if the stock falls below the 63 day average and
then rallies above it, the share is only likely to prove vulnerable
if it makes a new reaction low. If the share falls beneath its 63
day average and doesn't rally above it, then a prolonged period
of weakness is likely. In case anyone is getting confused over
which is the better average to use, it is a matter of personal
preference. I like to use a one year average for long-term work
because it changes direction less often than an average covering
a shorter period. But there are people who use one and a quarter
year averages as well. It is really a matter of personal preference.
If it works for you — use it.

JS *Presumably if a share breaks upwards through its moving average, that can be a buy signal?*

BM It is a good signal if a share breaks upwards through its moving average, but if the average itself is declining, the average, or the area on either side of it, may turn out to be a resistance area and block further progress.

JS *Does the share price have to break below the moving average for any length of time, or are just one or two days' confirmation sufficient?*

BM A length of time is often better than just one or two days, but sometimes one day is enough, especially with a big fall.

JS *How relevant is volume?*

BM I was brought up in the London stockmarket, where volume has only been available on individual shares in the comparatively recent past. I had to do without volume for a great deal of my career, so I am not a volume specialist. I would make the observation though that technical analysts have perhaps been even more successful in forecasting foreign exchange rates than in forecasting equity markets. And in the foreign exchange market, of course (with the exception of the IMM), no volume figures are available. So if technical analysts can survive in the foreign exchange market without volume, it does seem to me that that diminishes its worth in the reading of a share price chart.

One further point, or rather a joke may explain my attitude to volume: a broker rings his client and says, 'I have good news and bad news.' The client replies, 'Tell me the bad news.' The broker replies, 'The share that we bought at 50 is trading at 3,' to which the client replies, 'What's the good news?' Broker: 'It fell on low volume'.

Shares can fall on low volume, and they can rise on low volume as well. The former is supposed to be good news and the latter, bad, but neither cope with the fact that the share has undoubtedly moved one way or the other.

JS   *Are moving averages too slow a way of anticipating market movements? Is there a more prescient method?*

BM   Moving averages are slow — they are a confirming rather than a leading indicator. Momentum, on the other hand, frequently leads the market.

JS   *Do you mean by 'momentum', the rate of change?*

BM   Yes — the percentage rate of change.

JS   *Where can investors easily obtain charts that show moving averages?*

BM   Charts with moving averages are sold by a number of firms, such as Investment Research of Cambridge Ltd.

JS   *Everyone has heard of a head and shoulders pattern. Is this always a bearish sign?*

BM   Not at all. A head and shoulders can occur at the top of the market and at the bottom, when it is called a head and shoulders reversal. There is also a head and shoulders consolidation pattern where the market, having moved in one direction, pauses, forms the pattern, and then continues in the same direction.

JS   *What are the other well-known signals? Is a double bottom meaningful for instance?*

BM   A double bottom is meaningful and, like the head and shoulders pattern, also permits a precise calculation to be made of where the share is going. As far as other signals are concerned, triangles do frequently appear both as reversal and consolidation patterns.

JS   *What signs, signals or patterns should investors look for when buying a stake in a dynamic growth share?*

BM   A steeply rising relative and absolute price curve.

JS   *Presumably the patterns you would look for in an asset situation or a turnaround or cyclical stock would be very different. Could you elaborate on this?*

BM   Asset situations and turnaround or cyclical stocks are far more likely to form base areas such as a head and shoulders reversal or a double bottom. I remember during the great bear market of the early 1970s that Albright and Wilson made a very wide double bottom and broke out of the pattern on the bullish side while the market was still going down. Naturally it also showed good relative strength.

DOUBLE BOTTOM 1973 – ALBRIGHT & WILSON

SOURCE: INVESTMENT RESEARCH OF CAMBRIDGE LTD.

JS   *Is it fair to say that relative strength works best in a bull market and can be dangerous in a bear market?*

BM   Yes. Everything works better in a bull market and can be dangerous in a bear market — it is always dangerous to ignore the price chart itself. In a bear market a share might show excellent relative strength while falling, albeit falling less than the market itself. In this case relative strength would be positively misleading, whereas a price chart ought to help the investor to avoid the worst pitfalls.

JS   *Have you any other general tips or advice on charts, especially for dynamic growth shares?*

BM   A dynamic growth share is clearly going to show a steeply rising curve on its chart, and the longer that trendline has been in existence, the more important it becomes when the trendline is broken. For example, Poseidon, presumed to be a dynamic growth share in early 1970, had held above its original price

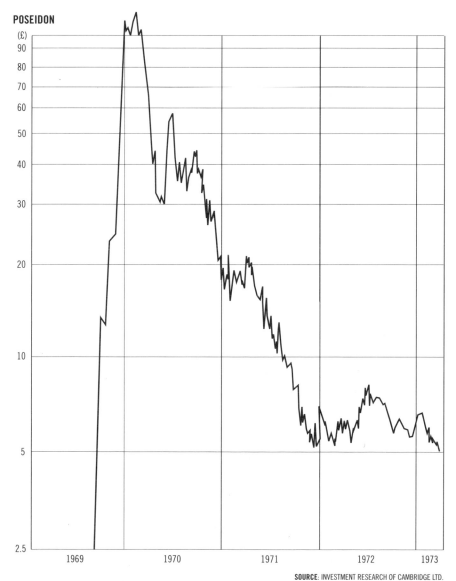

POSEIDON

SOURCE: INVESTMENT RESEARCH OF CAMBRIDGE LTD.

uptrend for a very long time. As soon as the uptrend broke, the share, having no nearby support because of the lack of long consolidation periods on the way up, had nowhere to go but down, back to where it came from.

JS   *I remember Poseidon very well.*

Brian Marber concluded by telling me a cautionary tale about relative strength. One day a surgeon walked into the terminal ward, situated on the tenth floor of a hospital. The patients were surprised to see him open the window and jump out. On the way down, the surgeon felt well, relatively speaking, compared with the way he felt when he hit the pavement. One of the patients, already confirmed as a terminal case, felt relatively better than the surgeon, when he saw him jump out of the window. A few days later the patient died anyway. The moral is clear — relying on relative strength is all very well provided that you do not die in the process.

We have only skated over the surface with a few thoughts on technical analysis. If you are further interested, an excellent book has been written on the subject — *Technical Analysis of Stock Trends*, which I refer to in detail under recommended reading in Chapter Sixteen. Meanwhile, I suggest that you use Datastream charts of relative strength and my 15% rule. Also remember that you should watch the relative strength of shares after you have bought them in case they are performing weakly. The price action may be sending you a warning signal about some bad news that is on the way.

9

—

OTHER CRITERIA

THE MAIN CRITERIA FOR SELECTING SMALL DYNAMIC GROWTH COMPANIES HAVE BEEN EXPLAINED IN DETAIL IN EARLIER CHAPTERS. Those that remain will be dealt with in this one:

SMALL MARKET CAPITALISATION

It is a fact of life that elephants don't gallop and small companies have much greater scope for future growth than very large ones. Wiles Group, capitalised at under £2m, had far more percentage upside potential than Hanson has at over £10bn. Some of today's very small companies will become the Hansons, Glaxos and Tomkins of tomorrow.

Although I mentioned earlier a limit of £100m market capitalisation, I would be very happy to increase this to £200m or more if all of my other criteria were satisfied. The £100m limit is more a matter of preference than necessity and is far from being carved in stone.

DIVIDEND YIELD

I prefer companies to pay a dividend, as most institutions need an income stream from their investments. Also, the dividend payment and forecast (if any) to some extent corroborate the management's confidence in the future. The ideal company will have a steadily increasing dividend growing broadly in line with earnings.

When you have found a company that can employ capital at say 20% per annum, you are really much better off if it retains the profits. You should not worry therefore if your dividend is small, provided it is well covered. With the right company, future growth in earnings and capital value will stem from earnings (less dividends paid) being ploughed back into the business and employed at an exceptionally high rate of return.

Any reduction in a company's dividend is a major event, with serious implications for the share price. By the time the announcement is made much of the damage will have been done. Fortunately, you will usually have some kind of advance warning that the dividend is threatened, and my advice is to sell your shares at the first hint of trouble.

REASONABLE ASSET POSITION

SPEYHAWK'S CANNON BRIDGE
DEVELOPMENT

There is a special chapter on value investing which deals with assets in much more detail. When investing in growth shares, assets are of limited importance. Property companies, like Speyhawk and Rosehaugh, that appeared to have substantial asset values, have all but melted away in the recession. In June 1992, Speyhawk has just written off £205m from the property values in its last set of accounts. Conversely, Cadbury Schweppes and Unilever have wonderful international brand names in their balance sheets at a fraction of true worth.

Any company that is growing reliably and well will tend to have an above average P/E ratio that will result in the shares being priced at well above asset value. The more a company earns on capital employed, the higher the growth rate and the higher the P/E ratio and the consequent premium of the share price over the asset value. With a super-growth stock, at a certain point, tangible assets become almost irrelevant. Does it really matter if Rentokil has assets representing only a small fraction of its share price? No-one is bothered about the assets per share, nor are they ever likely to be, provided the company has sufficient working capital, is not being over-geared and has a relatively strong balance sheet. You only need to know that the company of your choice can keep on doing its thing — growing at an above average rate.

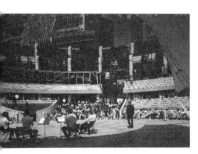

ROSEHAUGH'S BROADGATE
DEVELOPMENT

MANAGEMENT SHAREHOLDINGS

I like the Directors to own a number of shares substantial enough to give them the 'owner's eye', but not so many that they have control, can sit back and could at some future stage block a bid. The important point is for the shareholding to be significant to the Director in question. I like to see a good cross-section of the Directors with reasonable shareholdings and I always worry if the Finance Director is not among them.

Directors' sales are of great interest. The Finance Director selling 10,000 from his shareholding of 15,000 would be an obvious cause for concern. The founder or major shareholder selling a few shares would not worry me — he has to live. If, however, he sold half of his shareholding, that would unnerve me. I love to see more than one Director buying, especially those actively involved in the management of the company which pays their salaries.

There is an excellent publication, *Directus*, which gives details of Directors' sales and purchases as soon as they become public knowledge. Your broker will almost certainly subscribe to this or to a similar service and should be able to advise you about any significant movements in the shares of companies you have under scrutiny.

Now that you have a better idea of all the criteria for investing in small dynamic growth companies, we will move on to establish the weight that you should attribute to each of them.

10

WEIGHTING THE CRITERIA

I WILL RESTATE THE CRITERIA FOR SELECTING SMALL DYNAMIC GROWTH SHARES BEFORE WE ASSESS THEIR RELATIVE IMPORTANCE:

1. A positive growth rate in earnings per share in at least four of the last five years.
2. A low price earnings ratio relative to the growth rate.
3. An optimistic chairman's statement.
4. Strong liquidity, low borrowings and high cash flow.
5. A substantial competitive advantage.
6. Something new.
7. A small market capitalisation.
8. High relative strength of the shares.
9. A more than nominal dividend yield.
10. A reasonable asset position.
11. Management should have a significant shareholding.

The first criterion is very important: the five year record provides the back-cloth against which next year's growth in earnings will help the company to be seen in a more favourable light, which in turn facilitates a status change in the multiple. There is, however, no need to be absolutely dogmatic about the five year record — a shorter period will

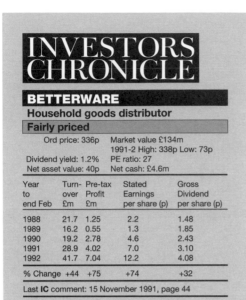

INVESTORS CHRONICLE

BETTERWARE

Household goods distributor

Fairly priced

Ord price: 336p	Market value £134m		
	1991-2 High: 338p Low: 73p		
Dividend yield: 1.2%	PE ratio: 27		
Net asset value: 40p	Net cash: £4.6m		

Year to end Feb	Turn-over £m	Pre-tax Profit £m	Stated Earnings per share (p)	Gross Dividend per share (p)
1988	21.7	1.25	2.2	1.48
1989	16.2	0.55	1.3	1.85
1990	19.2	2.78	4.6	2.43
1991	28.9	4.02	7.0	3.10
1992	41.7	7.04	12.2	4.08
% Change	+44	+75	+74	+32

Last **IC** comment: 15 November 1991, page 44

Betterware has turned in an astonishing performance since 1989 and the latest figures look equally impressive against a background of recession in the UK. Growth has come from increasing the geographic coverage of its core door-to-door sales operation. Although the average spend per customer has fallen from £9 to £7, recruitment of sales distributors, who are paid on a commission-only basis, has continued to rise. The group's foray into France is in its early stages and isn't likely to make a profit this year, although the longer-term potential looks promising and a former Avon executive has been re-cruited to take care of European expansion. The shares are highly rated and are difficult to deal in. **Most of the potential is now in the price.**

suffice if there has been a recent sharp acceleration in earnings growth from an easily identifiable source. Some of the best bargains are found when smooth earnings growth has been temporarily interrupted.

Examine the *Investors Chronicle* review of the 1992 results of Betterware, for example. 1989 seemed to spoil the record but £1.8m pre-tax was made by continuing activities and £1.25m was lost by discontinued activities giving the net result of £550,000 before tax. Betterware's record has been fantastic ever since, and in June 1992 the shares more than justified their very high multiple. There are many other similar instances. You must not let a minor blip in the earnings record put you off buying a great growth share. It does not matter so much what happened four or five years ago. Of course, you look for a five year record, but be prepared to be very flexible when the near-term record is excellent and the future forecast is very strong. This is where you should put the weight.

The second criterion, a low P/E ratio in relation to the growth rate, with a PEG factor below 0.75 and preferably below 0.66, ensures that the shares are being bought at a very attractive level. This makes a status change very likely. Buying shares with low PEGs also provides the investor with a *safety factor*. A share growing at 20% per annum on a multiple of 15 with a consequent PEG factor of 0.75 is obviously much safer to buy than a share growing at 15% per annum on a multiple of 30 with a PEG factor of 2.0.

The chairman's annual statement, and anything he says throughout the year, must be optimistic in tone, as otherwise future growth would be doubtful. If you find that the chairman is usually cautious, you can accept a mildly positive forecast from him. Any negative news or announcements should send you scuttling away to find another share.

Strong liquidity, low borrowings and high cash flow are of such importance, particularly in a recessionary climate, that I make the criterion mandatory. I have a degree of tolerance, however, particularly if the growth rate is exceptional and I can see that an uncomfortable liquid position will soon be eased by very high cash flow.

If a share fulfills all of my other criteria except competitive advantage, I usually soon realise that the company must have an advantage that I have failed to identify. A strong business franchise or niche business usually evidences itself by a relatively high rate of return on capital employed. My target figure is 20% per annum, which I am prepared to shade a little on occasions, but in most cases is mandatory.

It is important to understand that the first five criteria are the essence of the system and are all mandatory. The other criteria provide further *protection* helping to reduce the risk.

Let us examine the remaining criteria one by one and mark them on a scale of one to ten to give some idea of their relative importance. You will see how they interweave with each other to form a safety net under the already very conservative policy of only buying shares with a low PEG factor, a strong financial position and a competitive advantage:

BETTERWARE CATALOGUE

1. Something New

Very necessary when the earnings record is shorter than usual, as it helps to explain the reason for a sharp acceleration in earnings. Often a wonderful confirmatory bonus providing the reason for further upside in the share price and conversely reducing the downside.   *RATING 8*

2. Small Market Capitalisation

Increased upside potential, resulting in a better risk/reward ratio. You might be surprised, after all I have said to you about elephants not galloping, that a small market capitalisation is classified as important but not mandatory. If all my other criteria were met, I would be delighted to invest in a larger company, but finding a leading company that qualifies is unlikely as the FT-SE 100 Index shares tend to be exhaustively analysed by brokers and institutions. However, in the £100m to £300m bracket you will sometimes find a gem.   *RATING 7*

3. High Relative Strength

The high relative strength of shares substantially reduces the risk of there being any nasty surprises. Poor price action can sometimes give you a helpful warning signal to put you on red alert.   *RATING 6*

4. Dividend Yield

Always a comfort. On occasions dividend policy can be an early indicator of trouble ahead. *RATING 5*

5. A Reasonable Asset Position

A share with a low net asset value would obviously be less prone to a takeover, and in difficult times would have further to fall. *RATING 5*

6. Management Shareholding

To know that the Directors have their personal wealth at stake is a great comfort. Keeping a firm eye on Directors' dealings also protects your downside. *RATING 5*

The ratings are very arbitrary. They are not to be added up like a score but are simply to give you an idea of the relative importance to be attached to each of them.

I will now divide the criteria into three main categories:

1.	Five Year Record	
2.	Low PEG Factor	
3.	Optimistic Chairman's Statement	Mandatory
4.	Strong Financial Position	
5.	Competitive Advantage	
6.	Something New	
7.	Small market Capitalisation	Important
8.	Relative Strength	
9.	Dividend Yield	
10.	Reasonable Asset Position	Desirable
11.	Management Shareholding	

There can be little compromise on the first five criteria. With the second three, you might put up with one of them being very weak or even unfulfilled, provided all the other criteria were strongly in place. At the time of purchase, relative strength is the least important but subsequently is an excellent way of monitoring any weakness in the share price.

With the last three criteria, substantial compromises can be made as long as most other factors are in place. You always have to bear in mind that selecting a growth share is far more a question of judgement and feel than arithmetic. We will now examine a few real life examples from the past.

First, let us look at a May 1992 placing by stockbrokers, Panmure Gordon, of shares in Industrial Control Services Group plc. The stockmarket agreed with me that the placing price of 110p was on the low side — the shares opened in late May at 150p giving Panmure's clients an instant profit of about one-third on their initial investment. Not everyone is a Panmure client, so let us examine the shares at a price of 150p as they were quoted on the first day of dealings and see if they met my criteria:

AN ICS GROUP SAFTEY SYSTEM
UNDERGOING TESTS

1. Positive Five Year Record

1987	1988	1989	1990	1991
4.2p	0.4p	3.2p	4.5p	7.3p

As you can see there was a major set-back in 1988, but since then earnings have recovered well and in recent years have grown strongly. Not a five year record of growth, but the results for the first half of the year 1991/2 were already known and were very satisfactory. Within a few months the full year's results will be announced and the five year record will then be in place, though as a base year 1988 should be ignored.

2. Low P/E Ratio in Relation to Growth Rate

Forecast earnings were 9.1p for the year ending 31st May 1992. The difference between 9.1p and 7.3p is 1.8p, giving a growth rate for that year of 25%.

Now we come to a small complication - the earnings per share of 9.1p have to be adjusted downwards to allow for the impact of 50% of a subsidiary, ICS Bailey, being sold. It is made clear in the prospectus that ICS Bailey's contribution to the £4.5m profit forecast was £1.19m before tax. Half of this will be lost after the sale, reducing the after tax forecast from £2.94m to £2.54m, giving revised earnings per share on the adjusted average weighted capital of 7.7p. However, no allowance was made for any income from the cash to be received for their 50% of ICS Bailey, and profit forecasts for prospectuses so near to the end of the financial year are usually conservative, so I feel very comfortable with 8p EPS for the purpose of calculating the P/E ratio.

As the last month of Industrial Control Systems' financial year is May, it is reasonable to work on a 1992/3 prospective price earnings ratio. In the growing market for safety systems, you could reasonably anticipate that growth would continue at the same rate of 25% per annum for the next few years. This would lift earnings of 8p to 10p giving a prospective 1992/3 multiple of 15 at a price of 150p. The prospective PEG is therefore 25 (the growth rate) divided into 15 (the prospective multiple) — an attractive 0.60.

3. Optmistic Chairman's Statement

You already know from the placing particulars that the profits for the half year ended 30th November 1991 were well on course. Under the heading of 'Prospects', you learn that 'The Directors believe that the potential for further growth is excellent.' You also note that the safety systems market, which is in excess of $750m, is growing at about 10% per annum and in the UK a number of new electricity generation projects have been announced which should benefit the group. Coupled with the recent record, this is enough.

COMPUTER-AIDED DESIGN FACILITY
AT ICS GROUP

4. Strong Liquidity, Low Borrowings and High Cash Flow

After the placing, net tangible assets will exceed £16.6m. The total of bank overdrafts, commitments under hire purchase and finance leases and mortages less cash in hand will be just over £6.9m making net debt about 40%. The quick ratio will be 1.15:1.00. Neither are very attractive but they are passable.

5. Competitive Advantage

The ICS Group is a technical leader in the growing safety industry. Major installations have been completed for such important customers as British Gas, BP, Exxon, Shell, Chevron and Total. Operating profits were running at just over 10% of turnover in 1991 and the return on capital employed in that year was over 25%.

6. Something New

The Offshore Safety Act 1992 gave new regulatory power to the Health and Safety Executive and increased penalties for breaches of off-shore safety regulations.

7. Small Market Capitalisation

At 150p the market capitalisation was just under £60m. Well within our limit.

8. High Relative Strength

If the opening price in comparison to the placing price was anything to go by, the future relative strength of the shares should be excellent.

9. Dividend Yield

The yield at 150p is an acceptable 3.2%.

10. Reasonable Asset Position

The net assets of just under one-third of market capitalisation are not attractive in their own right but provide a small degree of comfort.

11. Management Shareholding

Directors will own over 60% of the shares after the placing. Not ideal, but acceptable.

ICS shares are a buy, as they fulfill most of the criteria of my system and, in particular, the prospective PEG is a very attractive 0.60. With the safety business in mind, let us return to MTL Instruments and see how that company measures up to my criteria, after a massive price increase from 150p in March 1991 to 295p a year later and onwards to 340p in May 1992.

The record of earnings was over 20% compound during the previous five years. 1991 earnings were 16.6p per share. In May 1992 the consensus forecast of two brokers was for 1992 earnings of 18.3p — a gain of just over 10%. Taking the consensus figure, the prospective multiple at 340p is 18.6 times earnings. The PEG on a 10% growth rate would therefore be a very high 1.86, making the shares a clear sell.

However, I believe that MTL is a fine company, which with its splendid record should be given the benefit of the doubt. My own belief is that, as in the past, the brokers' forecasts will prove to be conservative, and a more likely earnings per share figure for 1992 will be 19p per share, giving a prospective multiple of 17.5 and a growth rate of 14.5%. This would bring the PEG down from 1.86 to 1.20. As you know, I believe that superb growth shares like MTL should remain a long-term hold through thick and thin, but a prospective PEG of 1.20

based on an optimistic assumption is a test of character that I would probably fail. Certainly at 340p, the shares cannot be a buy in comparison with other growth companies, which are ripe for the same kind of status change that MTL has already enjoyed. On the other hand, MTL is a classic growth company which I would always keep under review, waiting for a better moment to repurchase.

Let us look at another share, Victaulic, which makes those yellow pipes you have often noticed stacked by the side of the road waiting to be laid. The gas and water industries are its main customers. The record of earnings growth has been excellent in recent years as evidenced by the article in the *Investors Chronicle* dated 6th March 1992.

The industry is relatively recession-proof and cash balances are strong but the forecast of future profits is only £15.5m, meaning that the growth rate is slackening. More recently, in April 1992, *The Estimate Directory* shows a consensus of ten brokers forecasts of £15.9m. Taking this figure, there would be an increase of £1.6m over the previous year's total of £14.3m, showing growth of 11%. After allowing for tax on the £15.9m, the prospective multiple would be approximately 16. The prospective PEG would then be calculated by dividing 11 (the growth rate) into 16 (the prospective multiple), resulting in a lofty PEG of 1.45. Far too high — an excellent share maybe, but with an insufficient safety margin for our system.

INVESTORS CHRONICLE

VICTAULIC
Plastic pipe and fitting maker
Fairly priced

Ord price: 769p	Market value £168m
	1991-2 High: 769p Low: 403p
Dividend yield: 2.5%	PE ratio: 18
Net asset value: 172p	Net cash: £9.7m

Year to 31 Dec	Turn-over £m	Pre-tax Profit £m	Stated Earnings per share (p)	Gross Dividend per share (p)
1987	51.8	6.5	21.9	10.0
1988	62.9	7.6	25.2	11.3
1999	78.3	8.8	28.8	13.0
1990	99.6	11.5	34.9	16.0
1991	115.0	14.3	42.5	19.6
% Change	+15	+25	+22	+23

Last **IC** comment: 25 August 1991, page 35

Another excellent result from Victaulic, boosted by rising capital spending at UK water companies. It's the dominant supplier of pipes, joints and fittings to the recession-resistant water and gas industries, which take 78 per cent of its sales. Last year saw increasing use of the new Excel high performance pipe and a move by water customers to longer, three-year contracts. Margins improved half a point to 12.2 per cent and strong cash flow eliminated debt. Brokers this year expect profits of at least £15½m, bringing the PE ratio down to 16 – justified while water company spending is still building up, but longer term Victaulic has to attempt diversification to keep the momentum going. At an all-time high but still **good value.**

Now, I suggest we re-visit Sage to see if after such astonishing growth that company measures up to our criteria today. You will remember that Sage's shares were a buy at 203p and by May 1992 they had risen to 469p. At this much higher level are they a buy, a hold or a sell? For a change, this time I will show an extract from the May 1992 *Estimate Directory*, which gives most of the information needed to make a judgement.

THE SAGE GROUP PLC
Ordinary shares of 5p

Price 477p
Market cap. £96m

SEDOL 0766960 EPIC SAGE SEAQ 52309

Activities The development and publication of business software for personal computers and the sale of computer stationary and supplies.

	Notes	Date of Forecast	PBT	9/92F EPS	DPS	PBT	9/93F EPS	DPS
BZW	B	14/4/92	8.7	29.1	9.00	10.0	33.1	10.00
County NatWest	B	24/4/92	9.0	30.2	9.00	10.5	35.0	10.50
Matheson	H	30/3/92	8.1	27.0	9.00	9.1	30.5	10.00
Panmure Gordon	B	10/2/92	8.4	29.3	9.25	-	-	-
UBS Phillips & Drew	-	23/4/92	9.0	30.9	9.00	10.5	36.2	10.00
Warburg	H	5/3/92	8.5	30.2	9.00	9.4	33.5	10.00
Wise Speke	LTB	24/4/92	9.0	30.1	9.50	10.1	32.8	10.40
Consensus			8.7	29.5	9.11	9.9	33.5	10.15
% change on previous year			+31	+16	+13	+15	+13	+11
Prospective P/E and DY on consensus				16.1	2.5		14.2	2.8

Major Shareholders

A Wylie	13.44%
A Goldman	10.51%
Lever P	7.78%
Morgan Grenfell Group	4.26%
Fmr Corp	4.12%
Framlington Group Plc	3.22%
Standard Life	3.18%
Norwich Union Life	3.04%

Year ended 9/91

PBT	6.6	P/E	18.7	
EPS	25.5	Dividend Yield	2.2	
Tax Charge	29			
Net Dividend	8.05			

Price Relative

1m	+2%
3m	+17%
12m	+90%

Announcements

Interims	14/4/92
Finals	10/12/91
Report and Accounts	27/1/92
AGM	20/2/92

As you can see, the phenomenal growth rate of the recent past seems to be slowing down. The brokers' consensus forecast for the year ending September 1992 is earnings per share of 29.5p making the growth rate for that year 16%. However, the half-yearly results announced in April led me to a different conclusion. In 1991, the first half showed EPS of 11.6p followed by 13.9p in the second half, to give a total of 25.5p for 1991. The first half of 1992 showed EPS up 25% at 14.5p with a recent US acquisition, DacEasy, making its first full six months' contribution. I suspect that earnings for the second half will be up by at least 20%, giving 17.4p for the second half, and a total of 31.9p for 1992. As you will see, my estimate of 31.9p is above all of the brokers' estimates, so I will take the top forecast of 30.9p as my base for calculating that at 469p the shares are on a prospective 1991/2 P/E ratio of just over 15.

The future consensus forecast estimates indicate that 1993 EPS will be 33.5p with growth of 13% (excellent in a recession, but not for Sage). The brokers' forecasts made after the interim results were announced in April show a higher estimated average EPS for 1993 of 34.3p. However, I believe that as in the previous year the top forecast of 36.2p made by UBS Phillips & Drew will be more likely to prove correct. You will find that it usually pays to give the benefit of the doubt to great growth stocks, especially those, like Sage, that enjoy a rate of return on capital employed of well over 100%.

What does all this add up to? On the top forecast of EPS for 1992 we have a figure of 30.9p and for 1993 36.2p. The estimated growth in EPS of 5.3p is 17%. The prospective P/E ratio for 1991/2 is 15. The prospective PEG for 1991/2 is therefore 17 divided into 15, which is about 0.9. Not a system buy, but definitely a hold, especially bearing in mind the expenses of switching. Also, there is the benefit of the interest-free loan from the government of about 100p per share, enjoyed by shareholders who purchased their shares at 203p and have not yet sold them, and as a result have not had to pay capital gains tax on their profit.

Sage's financial year ends on 30th September. If the share price stays the same the market will begin to look at Sage on a prospective multiple for 1992/3 of about 13. With the growth rate for the year estimated at 17%, that would make the 1992/3 PEG a more attractive 0.75 — just a buy within our system. As I have illustrated in Chapter Three with the example of MTL Instruments, if you time your purchase well, a rapidly growing share can often be bought very cheaply just before the market's perception of the share moves from the historic to the prospective multiple. The only snag with this approach is that you lose more time than usual while you wait for the shares to appreciate in value, and you take two years' profits on trust instead of only one. If you wait for the results for the previous year to be announced, you only take a risk on the forecast profit. However, if you missed the boat previously with a share like Sage and you are prepared to take the risk on two forecasts, this approach can sometimes offer you an opportunity to climb aboard.

Let us look at The Body Shop, a great growth company that is frequently in the news and has been a very rewarding investment for the brave. If you had bought shares in the market immediately after the company obtained a quotation in 1984, you would have paid a premium of 50% over the offer for sale price. As the shares were floated on a prospective multiple of 24, that would have meant paying 36 times prospective earnings. There have been several scrip issues and rights issues since then, but you would have made over sixty times your money. The shares have always commanded a high P/E ratio and have always seemed expensive in relation to the market as a whole. However, in PEG

ANITA RODDICK
GROUP MANAGING DIRECTOR,
THE BODY SHOP

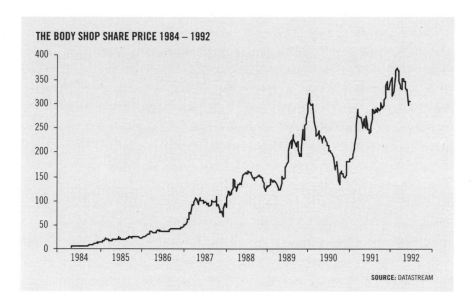

THE BODY SHOP SHARE PRICE 1984 – 1992

SOURCE: DATASTREAM

terms the shares have often been relatively cheap. After all, with a growth rate forecast at times to be as high as 50% per annum a prospective P/E ratio of 36 means that the PEG would be 0.72 and would fall just within our system. The difficulty of course is believing that a growth rate of 50% per annum can be maintained for any length of time.

The past is easy. Let us look at The Body Shop in July 1992. *The*

THE BODY SHOP INTERNATIONAL PLC
Ordinary shares of 5p

Price 278p
Market cap. £520m

SEDOL 0108313 EPIC BOS   SEAQ 50355

Activities The origination, production and retailing of naturally-based skin and hair care products and related items through its own shops and franchised outlets. As at Y/E 29/02/92 the group was trading from 210 stores in the UK and 517 stores overseas, an increase of 148 trading outlets internationally. The average number of employees during the Y/E 29/02/92 was 1,926 (1991: 1,844).

		Date of		2/93F			2/94F	
	Notes	Forecast	PBT	EPS	DPS	PBT	EPS	DPS
Beeson Gregory	B	28/5/92	32.5	11.4	2.00	40.0	14.5	2.40
Carr Kitcat	B	30/6/92	32.0	11.4	2.00	-	-	-
County NatWest	B	25/6/92	31.5	11.2	2.10	42.0	14.9	2.70
Fleming Securities	H	1/6/92	33.0	11.4	1.70	40.0	13.8	2.20
Girozentrale Gilbert Elliot	H	1/6/92	32.0	11.4	2.00	38.0	13.6	2.40
Hoare Govett	OV	28/5/92	31.5	11.1	2.00	38.0	13.5	2.45
James Capel	A3	29/6/92	32.0	11.0	2.00	41.0	14.3	2.50
Kleinwort Benson	-	29/6/92	32.0	11.3	2.00	37.0	13.0	2.25
Nomura	H	28/5/92	31.5	11.1	2.00	39.0	13.9	2.50
Panmure Gordon	B	3/6/92	33.0	11.5	2.10	42.0	15.0	2.70
Peel Hunt	-	13/2/92	34.0	12.0	2.25	-	-	-
S.G.S.T. Securities	H/B	29/6/92	31.1	11.0	2.00	40.2	14.2	2.40
Warburg	H	1/6/92	30.0	10.3	1.90	35.0	12.0	2.30
Williams de Bröe	B	28/5/92	34.5	12.4	2.20	47.0	16.8	3.00

Consensus

			32.2	11.3	2.02	39.9	14.1	2.48
% change on previous year			+28	+29	+26	+24	+25	+23
Prospective P/E and DY on consensus				24.6	1.0		19.7	1.2

Major Shareholders

I Mcglinn	27.97%
T Roddick	13.87%
A Roddick	13.76%

Announcements

Interims	12/11/91
Finals	27/5/92
Report and Accounts	10/6/92
AGM	30/6/92

Year ended 2/92

						Price Relative	
PBT	25.2	P/E	31.6			1m	-2%
EPS	8.8	Dividend Yield	0.7			3m	-19%
Tax Charge	34					12m	+12%
Net Dividend	1.60						

Estimate Directory shows the price at 278p, the consensus forecast of growth for next year at 29%, and on that assumption, a prospective P/E ratio of 24.6. The prospective PEG is calculated by dividing 29 into 24.6 giving 0.85, which is relatively attractive for a leading super-growth share.

The key point with The Body Shop is that the company's exceptional growth rate commands a high multiple. If you had bought the shares, you would have had a few uneasy moments when the Directors sold some of theirs and when there were bouts of unfavourable publicity. However, by and large you would not have seen the PEG move much above 1.2 until 1990, when growth flattened out temporarily.

The worry about buying a share like The Body Shop is that if growth suddenly stops the shares have a long way to fall, and there would be a rush for the exit. On the other hand, you cannot expect to multiply your money sixty times in a few years without taking some risk.

It is interesting to note that The Body Shop was a new issue of the last decade. Sage was a much more recent one. Both are exceptional growth shares starting as yearlings, one of which you hope will have the strength of character, ability and persistence to become another Red Rum.

There are still plenty of opportunities around in the new issue market. I have already mentioned ICS. Another recent issue was British Data Management which was placed by Rothschild in late March 1992 around the time of the General Election. The company appears to have the makings of an exceptional growth stock, so I suggest we analyse the statistics together in some detail. It is worth studying my approach, because, to justify buying the shares, you need to be a little inventive when dealing with the future growth rate and the PEG.

BDM is in the business of storage management and the distribution of commercial and oil exploration data. The group has 40% of the market for the fast growing oil and gas exploration industry, with important customers of the calibre of BP. Charges are made for annual storage and for the retrieval of documents when required. The service is very sophisticated and, needless to say, computer-based.

The issue was a flop because of uncertainty before the General Election, and the shares languished for some time under the issue price of 125p. Let us be conservative though and look at the numbers based on the issue price.

As you can see by studying the placing document, the year end is June, and on the Directors' forecast of £2.38m EPS are 10.9p. They do

EARNINGS AND PROFIT FORECASTS FOR THE YEAR ENDING 30TH JUNE 1992

(£000)	Directors' forecast	Pro forma forecast
Profit before interest and taxation	3,500	3,500
Net interest payable	(1,120)	-
Profit before taxation	2,380	3,500
Taxation	(490)	(850)
Profit after taxation	1,890	2,650
Number of Ordinary Shares (weighted)	17,262,398	23,262,398
Earnings per Ordinary Share (p)	10.9	11.4
Price earnings multiple at the placing price	11.4 times	11.0 times

however rise to 11.4p if, as you should, you adjust to assume that the issue had taken place at the beginning of the financial year. Let us now look at the recent record of profits and EPS growth:

TRADING RECORD AND PROFIT FORECAST

	Years ended 30th June			6 months ended 31st Dec	Forecast year ending 30th June
	1989 £'000	1990 £'000	1991 £'000	1991 £'000	1992 £'000
Turnover	8,131	11,155	12,679	6,203	
Profit/(loss) before interest	(253)	989	2,306	1,466	3,500
Net interest payable	(221)	(1,291)	(1,166)	(687)	(1,120)
Exceptional non-recurring items	(1,257)	-	-	-	-
Profit/(loss) before taxation	(1,731)	(302)	1,140	779	2,380
Taxation	311	-	45	10	(490)
Profit/(loss) after taxation	(1,420)	(302)	1,185	789	1,890
Earnings per share (p)	(9.3)	(2.0)	7.8	5.2	10.9

We would need a 1993 forecast to ascertain whether or not the shares fulfilled our most important criteria of a high future growth rate and a relatively low P/E ratio. We cannot let this company get away, so we have to improvise and make a few guesses. 1991 profits were more than double those of 1990, and 1992 profits were more than 50% up on 1991. The difference between the first half of 1991/2 of £1.46m and the forecast for the whole financial year of £3.5m is over £2m. Doubling that figure we arrive at £4m, and allowing for the next half year's growth we could safely add another £500,000 to give an estimate for 1992/3 of £4.5m.

In a similar way, I would calculate that 1993/4 profits would be about £5.5m. I know that I have not allowed for possible seasonal factors in the half year's results and that my approach is very rough and ready, but I am comforted by my liking for the business which seems to me to have excellent potential for further growth.

Now let us look again at the profits forecast of £3.5m for 1991/2 and the 11.4p of EPS shown in the placing document. As you can see from the profits record, there were substantial losses in the early years, giving rise to tax losses that were available to carry forward against future profits. The result is that the tax charge of £850,000 on the pro-forma forecast is abnormally low and the tax charge on the 1991 results was almost non-existent. The estimated tax charge for 1991/2 increased by £360,000, simply by adding the notional interest saving of £1,120,000 to profits. A normal tax charge is about one third, which in this case would have meant an extra £373,000 — very close to £360,000, clearly indicating that the tax losses have been used up and the company will in future be paying a normal tax charge.

BDM STORAGE FACILITY

If we assume a normal tax charge of one third for 1991/2 on the pro-forma profits of £3.5m, we will arrive at a net figure of approximately £2,335,000. There are going to be 23,262,398 shares in issue after the placing, so earnings per share amount to almost exactly 10p (It beats me why placing documents do not make this kind of thing *absolutely* clear). For 1992/3, our £4.5m estimate with a normal one third tax charge would give a net EPS figure of about 13p and for 1993/4 the £5.5m would give about 16p.

We now go back to the drawing board to calculate the PEG. As we are so near the end of the financial year and the company is fast-growing, I am going to use the prospective PEG for 1992/3. The estimated EPS are 13p a share, the issue price is 125p, so the prospective P/E ratio is about 10. The following year's growth is about 22%; the prospective PEG can therefore be calculated by dividing 22 into 10 to arrive at a very attractive 0.45.

The rest of the criteria are fine: there will be no debt after the placing, the company is well established in its industry, the rate of return on capital employed is a very satisfactory 22.5%, the new round of North Sea licencing was announced in March 1992, the market capitalisation at £29.1m is small and the dividend yield is 4.25%. Allowing for properties not being worth book value, net assets are about one third of the share price, and management has a substantial residual shareholding. The only criterion that is not satisfied is relative strength, which was poor. It is, however, easy to understand that the General Election would have affected sentiment, so I take this shortcoming with a pinch of salt.

I have dwelt at great length on BDM because, as you can see, I had to do some homework to find out if the shares were really a buy. There was the lesson of the abnormal tax charge, but more importantly the way to 'construct' the profit forecast and estimate the rate of future growth. Time will tell if my estimates are right. Barring accidents, I feel reasonably certain that they will prove to be conservative.

The most important single point to grasp is that it is difficult to find a share with a very low P/E ratio in relation to the growth rate. You will find a few each year by browsing through the *Investors Chronicle*, through recommendations from your broker and investment newsletters and by general reading. You will also find some excellent investments among new issues, which are often offered at a discount to normal market prices. However, as with BDM, you will sometimes have to work on the share a little before you can decide whether or not it is a system selection. This is especially the case with new issues, which frequently come to the market near to the end of their financial years. You may have to go forward a few months to anticipate how the shares will look then. You may have to do some work on the figures and take slightly more risk than you would normally like to bear, so that you can beat other investors to the punch. You will probably be selling by the time that they have fully realised the attractions of the share.

You will have noticed that I have been fairly dismissive about most of the criteria other than the mandatory ones. Once the attractive PEG is in place, the Chairman's forecast (or constructed forecast) is optimistic, and the company has a strong financial position and a high rate of return on capital employed, I begin to feel enthusiastic about the shares and take some persuading that I could be wrong. Strangely enough, most of the other criteria do usually drop into place. This is hardly surprising — if a company has a competitive advantage and something new has been happening, you would expect earnings growth to be exceptional.

Poor relative strength on its own should not put you off, but any weakness in the share price should alert you to the possibility that something *could* be going wrong. With an established growth stock, an indifferent net asset value is not a cause for concern. You should only begin to worry when a number of the non-mandatory criteria are not in place. Taken together they form a safety net, which will only break if *several* of the strands are frayed or missing.

11
———

CYCLICALS AND TURNAROUNDS

MOST COMPANIES BENEFIT FROM AN UPTURN IN THE ECONOMY AND SUFFER IF THE ECONOMY TURNS DOWN. However, a really great growth stock will usually manage to produce increased earnings even in the depths of a recession. Some companies with strong business franchises seem to be amazingly unaffected by the gloom and despondency around them. Cyclical stocks suffer much more than most — building and construction companies, steel companies and automobile manufacturers and distributors cannot buck the trend. The most they can hope to achieve is that at the top of the next cycle, they will be ahead of their previous peak, and at the bottom be better placed than last time around.

Hair-raising stuff, but there is plenty of money to be made if you can get your timing right. To do this you have to understand the anatomy of business cycles. Let us take housebuilding for example. At the bottom of the cycle a few survivors in the business will benefit from reduced competition and begin to turn the corner. They would be finding that prime land and labour were far easier to acquire and, therefore, much cheaper than during the boom. Fewer houses would be under construction, so the prices of those being sold would be more favourable to the builder, providing healthier margins and better profits. Other entrepreneurs aware of the growing opportunity would set up as builders or expand their existing building businesses and would compete for both labour and land. Cost pressures begin to increase. Some of the builders borrow to stock-pile land which is becoming more difficult to acquire and therefore more expensive. Very soon, there is over-capacity in the business, so some housebuilders slash prices to maintain market share. Margins erode due to lower prices and increased costs. The banks, fearing their loans are in jeopardy, foreclose on the more marginal businesses, which become bankrupt. Some of the more entrepreneurial builders decide that there may be better opportunities elsewhere. Competition falls away, pricing pressures ease and profits begin to improve. The cycle starts all over again.

Clearly, the time to buy is before profits rise and the time to sell is when conditions are obviously improving. The important point to grasp is that a cyclical stock should *never* command a very high multiple and a low dividend yield near to the top of the cycle. Let us look at GKN, a typical cyclical stock, to see how its profits and share price were affected by the last two business cycles.

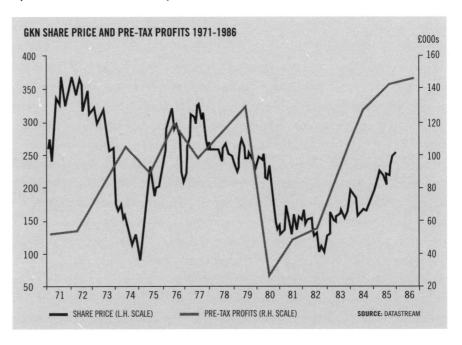

Obviously, you want to time your purchases so that you buy near the bottom of the cycle, but you also want to make sure that your selection is going to survive. Of course, you would enjoy a far bigger gain if you invested in an unlikely candidate for survival which surprised everyone by coming through the recession unharmed. The greater the risk, the greater the potential reward. The riskier companies usually have very high borrowings at the bottom of a cycle. When they run out of money, much may depend upon the attitude of their bankers and loan stockholders.

Here are some guidelines that should help you with your selections:

1. Companies with well-known, national names have a better chance of survival, if only because there seems to be greater reluctance to let them fail. They are an important part of the fabric of our society, so the bankers, loan stockholders and other creditors involved may stretch a few points to be helpful. In some cases, this may be to avoid the undesirable publicity of being accused of pulling the plug, and in others a genuine desire to help the company.

2. Usually, a company with a well-known name will have already attracted a stockbroker of high calibre and some strong institutional shareholders, who are more likely to help place stock to finance a reconstruction. You must make sure that the company stockbroker is a leading one.

3. Seek out companies with familiar brand names and other kinds of strong business franchises. Look particularly for those companies which usually have a high return on capital employed.

4. The calibre of management is obviously crucial. If the old guard remains totally in charge you should be more cautious. A change of management with someone able becoming Chairman or Chief Executive, obviously bodes well for the future and makes your investment a better bet.

5. Keep an eye open for major competitors going out of business. This is always a very good sign. Your selection should, as a result, be able to secure a larger and more profitable piece of the eventual pie.

6. Seek out companies with asset backing in excess of market price. These assets should help to generate earnings when the economy recovers. Meanwhile, they may catch the eye of a predator. With the hope of a takeover in mind, you should give preference to companies with a widely based shareholding and no control blocks.

7. As usual, there is no escape from a little arithmetic. What is the brokers' consensus forecast in the event of a recovery? What was the P/E ratio at the top of the last cycle? With these two figures in mind, you can easily calculate your potential upside, which for a company with containable borrowings (see 8. below) should be at least 100% and possibly much more.

8. The magic word 'borrowings' brings me to another important point. You should draw the limit at total indebtedness exceeding the net asset value. In other words, gearing should not be more than 100%.

    In the rare cases when you find that the rest of your criteria are overwhelmingly satisfied, you could stretch the 100% limit, but in that event you should be looking for upside potential in excess of 100%. The extra risk must be balanced by the promise of extra reward.

9. It is absolutely essential that the forecast for the year ahead shows rising profits or a return to profits. Losses could produce the kind of fatality you are seeking to avoid.

10. Timing is of the utmost importance. If someone throws a safe out of a window from the penthouse of a skyscraper, you will be severely damaged if you lean out of a window on the third floor and try to catch it. Wait until you are really sure that the cycle has hit bottom. You are looking for the first glimmer of a change — the first hint of good news after the gloom. You will pay a little more this way but look upon the extra cost as an insurance premium.

11. You want your selection to benefit massively from the upturn. Therefore, you need to ensure, as far as you possibly can, that the company's main infrastructure has remained intact throughout the recession. The brokers' consensus profit forecast reflects this in arithmetical terms, but here are a few further specific pointers:

    a) Ensure that the company has maintained capacity and that major factories have not been sold off.
    b) Look for turnover being largely upheld with only margins suffering. This is an excellent indicator as margins can recover quickly.

c) Check if there has been substantial cost cutting. You want your company to be lean and mean in the upturn.

d) Look for companies that are usually good cash generators. If tax losses are allowable for set-off against future profits, short-term debts could be repaid very speedily.

12. Directors' share dealings are very important when considering cyclical situations. Seeing a number of Directors buying shares near the low point of the cycle is obviously a very encouraging sign. They might be wrong, but they ought to know.

13. Buying at the time of a rights issue can be a very attractive way of participating in a recovery. You have the great advantage of being able to study an up-to-date circular to shareholders in which you can see what the Directors are doing with their entitlement, see how much debt remains, and obtain an instant fix on the outlook for future profits.

14. Above all, you are looking for a company that under normal conditions is a substantial force in its chosen field. One of the best measures of this is sales in relation to market capitalisation. Anything over five times is relatively cheap.

    Next is a good example. In 1985, sales were £146m and the market capitalisation was £195m. A sales to market capitalisation ratio of 0.75. By December 1990, the market capitalisation had slumped to £24m, although sales were forecast at £800m. The ratio of sales to market capitalisation had become a very attractive 33 times. In the event, the shares subsequently rose from 6.5p in December 1990, to 95p in June 1992.

When should you sell a cyclical? With a growth share you might stay to enjoy a long ride, but with a cyclical your target price tends to be more limited. You certainly sell immediately when you see press or broker comment suggesting that the company in question is a growth share. You also sell when the multiple on the forecast profit in the second year of recovery has risen to 75% of the highest multiple the company has ever achieved. In essence, you sell on general recognition that the company has survived the downturn and is now enjoying far better trading conditions. Do not wait until there is an inevitable increase in competition, costs are beginning to rise again and demand is on the

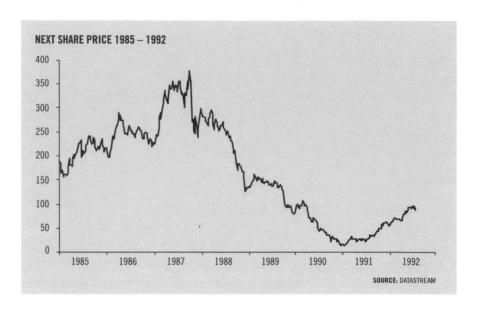

NEXT SHARE PRICE 1985 – 1992

SOURCE: DATASTREAM

brink of flagging. You are trying to operate with a substantial safety margin, so sell well before the top of the cycle.

Although I dislike arithmetical formulae for selling, I would also suggest that for anything other than a very highly geared situation (in which you took a substantial risk with the hope of a disproportionate reward) you should at least consider selling when the shares have doubled.

Now comes the more difficult question of how to cut losses. Remember you were only buying when you thought the cycle was turning up. If this has not happened and the cycle is still going down or you are disappointed in some other major way, you must obviously re-appraise the situation. As with all my other systems of investment, if the story has changed substantially for the worse, sell immediately. Inexplicable falls in price have to be assessed on their merits and become more a question of judgement and feel. I have covered this particular problem more fully in Chapter Seventeen on Portfolio Management.

I rarely invest in cyclicals as the upside seems to me to be limited to a one-off gain. There are, however, large profits to be made if you are expert in both timing and selection.

This is well illustrated by Next, which is worth studying in more detail. Although it was easy to miss investing at the low of 6.5p, there were several further opportunities a little later on in the saga. Along with most of the retail sector, Next over-expanded during the latter part of the eighties, adding to its chain of shops at a phenomenal rate and branching out into credit finance and mail order. By December 1988, the group warned of a coming 'significant drop in profits' and George Davies, previously a star in retailing, was asked to resign. By December 1990, investors were close to despair, with the company moving into heavy losses and with the prospect of two convertibles being near to redemption for £150m. By March 1991, Next had sold Grattan for £167m which, together with a few other minor sales, took the company out of debt. At that date, Next measured up to most of our criteria reasonably well:

GEORGE DAVIES

1. Next is a well-known company and would have been a very high profile failure had it been allowed to go under.

2. Next had a well-known and influential stockbroker.

3. Next is an excellent brand name.

4. George Davies had been replaced by David Jones and Lord Wolfson of Sunningdale, both of whom are very able, financially-orientated men, who were determined to restore Next's balance sheet to health.

DAVID JONES

5. Major competitors such as Burton were also under considerable pressure.

6. After the Grattan deal, debt was no longer a problem.

7. Losses stopped and improving profit forecasts became the vogue with brokers.

LORD WOLFSON

8. The intention was to restore the core business. Shops were being closed, stock controls improved, and product lines overhauled. Turnover was reduced in the process and margins improved dramatically.

9. The sales to market capitalisation ratio was still high. Even after the disposal of Grattan, sales were forecast at £450m. At 30p, the ratio was more than four times the market capitalisation of £110m.

The most obvious time to buy Next was after the sale of Grattan, when the fear of bankruptcy was removed. You could have bought the shares then for between 25p and 30p for several months, and by June 1992 you would have at least trebled your money.

Turnarounds are not far removed from cyclicals and asset situations. An asset situation that has been neglected for years and allowed to deteriorate to the brink of failure becomes a turnaround. A badly-managed cyclical often becomes a turnaround at the bottom of the cycle. A badly-managed growth company that experiences an unexpected disaster might also become a candidate.

There is no precise definition of a turnaround. I use the expression to describe a company that I hope is going to come back almost from the dead. A company that has been bewitched, battered and bewildered to such an extent that its capacity to survive is in real doubt. The market often exaggerates hopes on the way up and exaggerates fears on the way down. Frequently, a fall in share price can be overdone as institutions and other shareholders rush for the exit.

Most of the criteria for selecting a turnaround are the same as those I have suggested for a cyclical. Many turnarounds at their lows are suffering from a downturn in their own circumstances, sometimes less to do with their basic business than changes in management and direction. Really bad management can bring any company to its knees, and really good management can quickly put things right. You do not want to waste valuable time and risk precious money waiting for new management to arrive on the scene. A major change in management (for the better you hope) is usually an excellent buying signal, although sometimes things have to get worse before they can get better.

For example, let us examine that well-known company English China Clays, which for some inexplicable reason diversified away from a wonderful core business and decided to change its attractive name to the horrible acronym — ECC. A new chief executive, Andrew Teare, who had successfully run Rugby Group for several years, took charge on 1st July 1990. The acquisition of Georgia Kaolin in the US had already been announced in May, and Teare decided to use this purchase to build up the core business and dispose of all the previous diversifications. In September 1991, the company announced its gradual withdrawal from the UK housebuilding sector and a rationalisation programme in the core kaolin operation. Other changes included moving head office, introducing a wide-ranging management incentive scheme, selling ten businesses within eighteen months and cutting the workforce from 13,800 to 10,800. In February 1992, the company had a rights issue to redeem some fancy debt financing in the

U.S.A. A month later, the board announced pre-tax profits up more than 50% and proposed that the company's name should be changed back to the much more popular 'English China Clays.'

In July 1990, the shares were 414p, on a historic P/E of 9.2 and a prospective P/E of about 18. Towards the end of 1990, the shares were very weak at 275p as the company bore the brunt of worries about the recession in construction work. However, by June 1992 the shares reached 555p when the benefits of the reorganisation came through.

Another kind of turnaround can arise from unexpectedly horrific financial results or a disaster like the Union Carbide plant blowing up in Bhopal. I recommend against investing in turnarounds which arise from happenings that are impossible to quantify and may be a bottomless pit. The Bhopal incident has no doubt given rise to claims of unimaginable proportions from relatives of disaster victims. I am not sure about the present state of play, but I suspect that years may go by before the full financial effects will be known.

Similarly, if there is ever a case of a successful claim against a major tobacco company for damage to health of third parties from passive smoking (such as being in the same office as other people who are smoking and dying from cancer as a result) the effects would be immeasurable. With happenings like these, I suggest that you allow plenty of time for the dust to settle before you risk your money. Do not go bottom-fishing — you can drown that way.

As you can see from the examples of Next and English China Clays, there are very large gains to be made by identifying a promising cyclical or turnaround, especially when new management has taken charge. There is of course a risk, so you should never put more than 10% of your portfolio in any one situation of this kind. The safety criteria I have outlined should also help to protect you.

The time to sell a turnaround is delightfully obvious — when the company has turned around and is making good profits. Institutions are no longer ashamed to own the stock and are beginning to invest cautiously: the brokers' consensus profits forecast is well up on last year and there are perhaps a few comments about the company becoming recognised as a growth stock. Do not be greedy — let the market have your shares. You may well have made at least 100% on your money and possibly much more.

12

—

SHELLS

I ONCE COMPARED A VERY LARGE COMPANY WITH AN ELEPHANT BY MAKING THE COMMENT THAT 'ELEPHANTS DON'T GALLOP'. The main reasons are obvious — to double the size of a very large company capitalised at say £10bn takes years of hard work. A small and obscure company finds doubling much easier, and a shell company, with a market capitalisation of a few million, has an even easier task. I have searched for an analogy for shells to contrast with my elephant ambling along most of the time and just occasionally charging. The best suggestion I can offer so far is a flea, which can jump over two hundred times its own height — equivalent to a man jumping over St. Paul's Cathedral. Let us have a look at our flea in action and see how shells work and how you can benefit from the process.

A shell is a very small company that usually owns a small and nondescript business of little account and which, above all, has a stock market quotation. The idea of the incoming entrepreneur is simply to obtain a back-door quotation for his own company, which usually has too short a record or some other shortcoming that precludes obtaining a stock market quotation by a more conventional route. Often, the previous management makes a quick exit shortly afterwards and the original business is sold off as it becomes less relevant to the main activity of the new group. The incoming entrepreneur then has effective board control of the business together with the quotation he was seeking. The shares often rise in price sharply in the hope that there will be plenty of activity. Using the high-flying shares, the company then makes some acquisitions. The share price goes up again in anticipation of more action, and the process is repeated. That is the shell game at its best. The private investor benefits by being in the shell in the first instance, or shortly afterwards, by participating in one of the early placings of stock or by buying in the market.

To find out about companies that are likely to be used as shells or have just started their career as a shell, I recommend to you two newsletters that specialise in shell operations — *The Penny Share Guide* and *Penny Share Focus*. Both are helpful publications and review each month the progress being made by most shells. They also feature potential shells together with a wide range of other very small companies, often called penny stocks. Their comments will keep you abreast of the main developments on the shell scene. Another possible source of information is the *Fleet Street Letter*, which often mentions shells in its Portfolio C section, but concentrates in the main upon medium-sized to larger companies.

Your broker may also know of some interesting shells. Ask for his views — he will be anxious to help you. Newspapers, especially the Sundays and the *Daily Mail*, frequently comment on shells. Michael Walters, who is Deputy City Editor of the *Daily Mail*, has written a comprehensive book, *How to Make a Killing from Penny Shares*, which gives valuable advice and outlines the pitfalls. If you intend to concentrate upon shells, you should read this.

It is important to understand how an acquisitive shell can be such a good investment for early shareholders. Take the example of a property company (when they were all the rage) with one million shares in issue priced on the Unlisted Securities Market (USM) at 50p each, having a market capitalisation of £500,000. The net asset value might be only £250,000, and the 100% premium of £250,000 would be the hope factor — hope that the company will be used as a shell.

The incoming entrepreneur injects his own property business worth say £2m for 4 million shares. The result is a quoted property company with assets of £2.25m and 5 million shares in issue, so by strict arithmetic, if the share price remained at 50p the market capitalisation would by then be £2.5m. However, the accompanying publicity would probably boost the share price to say 100p, capitalising the company at £5m. This is a very small jump for our flea, as there are only one million shares from the original shell that form the market float, and many of these will be in the firm hands of believers and supporters. There might be only 200,000-300,000 shares that are available to the market, and these will usually be sold quickly at higher levels to new converts. The key to a successful shell operation is for there to be more demand for the shares than can be satisfied by the relatively limited supply. That is why very small companies make the best shells.

At this point, our shell makes a substantial acquisition with net assets of say £2.5m. The purchase consideration is satisfied by £1m in a deferred loan secured on the property, and the rest is funded by an issue of 1.5 million ordinary shares which are placed by the company's brokers with friends, business associates and institutions. The extra 1.5 million shares that are being issued will add to the float, but this problem will be restricted as in the early stages many of the placees will be friends and business associates who will hold the shares as a long-term investment.

The effect of all this is to increase net assets per share. There have been three distinct stages:

	Stage 1	Stage 2	Stage 3
Shares in issue	1m	5m	6.5m
Net assets	£250,000	£2,250,000	£3,750,000
NAV per share	25p	45p	58p

In the column for Stage 3 I have increased the net assets by £1.5m, which is the £2.5m of assets acquired less the £1m deferred loan. The sense of progress from the net asset growth from 25p to 58p per share will usually be accompanied by the feeling that the new £2.5m acquisition is very astute and that the property in question is really worth very much more, especially if planning permission can be obtained for an exciting new development.

I have given first the example of a property shell because the arithmetic with net assets is easier to follow than with earnings. In fact, earnings situations lend themselves to shell operations much more readily, as future earnings estimates are essentially hopes that may or may not be realised. Taking a similar example with an industrial company, shares would be issued on a high P/E ratio for profits valued on a lower multiple. Let us assume that the same initial shell company had £250,000 worth of assets which could be converted into cash yielding £25,000 per annum. The incoming entrepreneur reverses in his business for the same 4 million shares, but instead of his business having assets of £2m, there are profits of £300,000 per annum before tax. In anticipation of deals to come and hopes for the future of the underlying business, the shares again double to a pound. Then another business is purchased for the same £2.5m, but in this case the profits before tax are £400,000 per annum. Again the vendor agrees to £1m of deferred consideration, and the balance is satisfied by the issue of 1.5 million new shares of £1 each. Our three stages look like this:

	Stage 1	Stage 2	Stage 3
Shares in issue	1m	5m	6.5m
Profits before tax per annum	£25,000	£325,000	£625,000
Pre-tax earnings per share	2.5p	6.5p	9.6p

Tax has been ignored, as rates vary for companies at lower levels and I do not want to complicate the issue. I have deducted £100,000 per annum from profits to allow for interest on the deferred consideration. The £625,000 pre-tax profits per annum figure is the sum of £25,000 plus £300,000 plus £400,000 less £100,000. You will readily appreciate that as a result of the takeover of the shell and the first acquisition, the earnings per share on a pre-tax basis rose dramatically from 2.5p to 6.5p and finally to 9.6p. Shareholders' pre-tax earnings per share almost quadrupled. In addition, as more acquisitions in the same industry are made, there will be scope for rationalisation and, in some cases, for radical improvement by re-organisation. Plenty of new hope — the raw material of a high multiple.

You should be aware that, with a highly acquisitive company, there is also the likelihood of profit enhancement by creative accounting. For example, by writing down the cost of acquisitions, capital can be transmuted into future revenue profit. Another simple ploy would be for the shell company to pay a little more for the business it is acquiring and arrange for the deferred loan to be interest-free. This would add £100,000 per annum to pre-tax profits. Very acquisitive companies frequently do this kind of thing, so bear in mind that often their profits are not all they seem to be at first sight. Not many people read the small print.

Investing in shells is more of an art than a science. To decide whether a company is a shell or simply a very small business with a quotation is very much a matter of opinion. The key point is that whoever is reversing their business into the company invariably takes board control, and their underlying motive is to obtain a back-door quotation. In some cases the original business may be retained and developed. To find a worthwhile asset inside a shell is a bonus for the incoming entrepreneur, rarely his reason for doing the deal.

One of the Oxford dictionary definitions of the word shell is *'Unimportant firm made the subject of a takeover bid because of its status on the Stock Exchange'*. Another more pertinent meaning is *'outward show, mere semblance'*.

To give you a better idea of both the attractions and the dangers of shells in the last twenty years, let us look at four well-known examples and see how they have fared in the market.

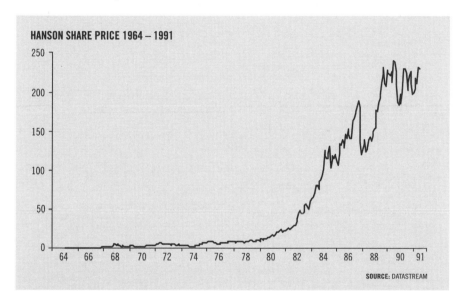

HANSON SHARE PRICE 1964 – 1991

SOURCE: DATASTREAM

LORD HANSON

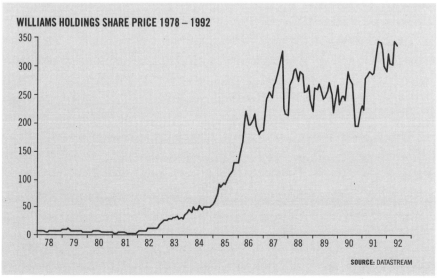

WILLIAMS HOLDINGS SHARE PRICE 1978 – 1992

SOURCE: DATASTREAM

BRIAN McGOWAN   NIGEL RUDD
CHIEF EXECUTIVE   CHAIRMAN

133

ASIL NADIR
FORMER CHAIRMAN, POLLY PECK

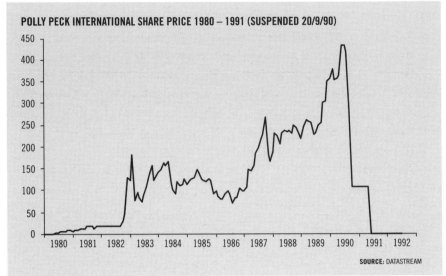

ROGER FELBER
FORMER CHAIRMAN, PARKFIELD

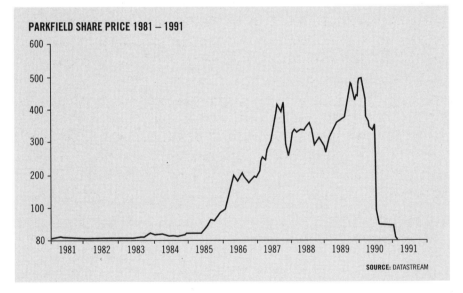

You can invest in shell companies at four distinct stages of their development, when:

1. They are waiting for a deal but there is nothing in sight.
2. A deal is rumoured and speculation is beginning.
3. A deal is announced and the company returns to the market.
4. The new managers have been operating for a few months or even longer and are beginning to show their paces.

The first two stages are too nebulous and dangerous for most investors. You are quite likely to invest inadvertently in a genuine company in distress which will soon become insolvent. Alternatively, you might have a very long wait for new management to arrive and take control. Therefore, I recommend that you concentrate upon the last two methods so that, when you invest, you will know for certain that the company is being used as a shell. You will know the name and background of the incoming entrepreneur and have a firm idea of his objectives and the fundamentals of the company. A number of uncertainties will have been removed.

After the successful reversal of the new business into a shell company, the shares are invariably suspended for about six weeks. During this time a prospectus is prepared setting out details of the deal, which also often includes a placing of more shares for cash. When the shell returns to the market, the fundamentals tend to be ignored and the opening market price is usually related to the pre-suspension price. For example, if a company's shares have an underlying value of 5p and are suspended at 8p, you might well hear that the shares 'have a 10p look about them'. With a shell, fundamentals like assets and earnings per share are frequently of lesser importance. Much more attention is rightly focused upon the new man at the helm, his track record, his backers and what he is likely to achieve by acquisition, rationalisation and the occasional spectacular deal.

Another way for an entrepreneur to move into a shell is simply by invitation. A substantial shareholder with effective board control might invite a well-known personality to become chief executive. Shortly afterwards, there would be a rights issue and placing to give the new man a chance to acquire a significant shareholding. He would also be rewarded and incentivised with share options.

To give you the full flavour of the different methods of acquiring control of a shell, let me show you details of three recent shell operations:

1. CLARKE FOODS

An American businessman, Henry Clarke, together with his family, acquired effective control of Yelverton Investments — a small investment company which he turned into a cash shell. In 1991, he acquired the ice cream businesses of Hillsdown Holdings and Lyons Maid from Allied Lyons. Although trading profits are still awaited, overnight the company became a leading UK manufacturer and distributor of quality ice cream. Before the venture into ice cream was announced, the shares were 39p; by June 1992, they had risen to about 150p.

CLARKE'S ICE-CREAM

2. MADDOX GROUP

In February 1992, Hugo Biermann and Julian Askin alighted upon Pathfinders and injected two telephone cable businesses for cash and shares, acquiring in the process a 26% stake in the company, which was re-named Maddox Group. The two men had previously turned Thomson T-line from a £900,000 company into a group they sold to Ladbroke for over £180m. Shares in Pathfinders /Maddox rose after the announcement to 12.5p, though they have slipped back to 8p in June 1992 as the market waits for another deal.

3. WHARFEDALE

In December 1991, Wharfedale announced that a new management team was moving in headed by Sir Gordon Brunton, who had sixteen years as Chief Executive of the International Thomson Organisation, during which time annual operating profits increased from next to nothing to over $500m. Other members of the team were Pieter Totte and Gordon Owen, who was Group Managing Director of Cable and Wireless.

SIR GORDON BRUNTON

At the same time, the company indicated that there would be a £2.25m placing of shares at 12.5p to repay some of Wharfedale's excessive debt. At the annual meeting in March 1992, the management outlined their plans for reorganising the business and gave details of their progress on cost-cutting and rationalisation. The market price has been as high as 24p but by June 1992 had dropped back to 16p to await further developments.

As you can see, all three of these companies are priced on expectations of things to come. In contrast, a new issue of a straightforward business might be valued strictly on fundamentals like the growth rate, current earnings per share, the forecast, the P/E ratio, asset backing, dividend yield and liquidity. You will readily appreciate that giving you guidelines for judging the value of a shell and selecting a suitable one to add to your portfolio is almost impossible. I say 'almost' because I am going to try:

1. First, second and third is the provenance of the incoming management. Look for quality. Look for a heavyweight board joining a lightweight company. Look for previous positive achievement upon which to build your future hopes. Full details of the incoming management should be contained in the prospectus, and there will usually be plenty of press and newsletter comment

about any well-known personality.

Your new chief executive may not have run a company of his own before — he could have been working for another well-known group for many years. An excellent stable is one of the best auguries.

Before Greg Hutchings joined F.H. Tomkins he worked as head of UK corporate development at Hanson Trust. When he first became Chief Executive of Tomkins the shares were 12p with a capitalisation of £6m. In June 1992, the shares stand at just under 500p with a market capitalisation for the company of £1.4bn. After making allowance for rights and scrip issues, Tomkins' shareholders have enjoyed an enormous capital gain so far, and Greg is still going strong.

Bernard Taylor was chief executive of Glaxo before he joined Medeva. The shares were 80p at the time and in June 1992 less than three years later stood at 220p, a gain of 175%. Hanson and Glaxo are obviously top class stables, but there are other similar shell situations in which you can tell that the odds are very much in your favour.

I have dwelt at length upon the desirability of top quality management for a shell because that criterion is far more important than all of the others. If the incoming entrepreneur is absolutely first class, the rest of the criteria should be given much less weight.

2. As an important adjunct to my first criterion, I like to make sure that the new management is buying a substantial stake in the company. This is almost always the case, but keep a close eye on Directors' buying and selling and regard substantial selling as a clear signal to do the same, almost irrespective of any accompanying explanations.

3. As the future progress of the shell will depend to a large extent upon share placings, the calibre of the company's stockbroker, merchant banker and investing institutions is a material consideration. A first class incoming executive team will usually attract substantial support.

4. The record of the business being reversed into the shell has to be one of increasing profits and earnings per share, unless of course it is a property company, when different considerations apply. If the new Chief Executive is relatively unknown, the record of the business he has been managing is often the only way for you to

judge past achievements.

5. Make sure that, following the merger, the shell has resultant earnings per share sufficient to provide a reasonable starting base for the company. You cannot use the PEG factor to measure the price you are paying. You have to take a broader view with shells, but at your entry price try to avoid paying too much for hope.

It is the absolute amount of the premium over real value that should worry you, not the percentage. This is of course another argument in favour of small shells. For example, if a shell company has profits after tax of £200,000 and the multiple for that type of business would normally be 15, the company would be capitalised at £3m. However, with the hope factor for a really good new Chief Executive, the multiple might be as high as 25, capitalising the company at £5m. The extra £2m is a premium of 66.7%, but really you should not focus on the percentage but on the £2m which is the 'hot air gap' that has to be replaced with value. With a high P/E ratio and good backing it would not be too difficult. Now let us contrast this with a company capitalised at £50m with true worth of only £30m. Closing a hot air gap of £20m, with the same percentage premium, would be a far more onerous task for the incoming management, especially as they would also have to worry about a much larger market float of shares.

6. From the above comparison, you will readily appreciate that a little shell, capitalised at £1m and with an underlying business worth £500,000, might be a gem. A 100% premium, but a hot air gap of only £500,000. I very much prefer small companies. I like a shell with a starting market capitalisation of under £10m. The smaller the better — remember our flea.

It is very instructive to note the history of Wassall. Christopher Miller and Philip Turner, who had been key executives of Hanson, joined the board of Wassall plc together with a business associate David Roper from Dillon Read. There was an immediate rights issue, and institutions came in heavily, together with Hanson, which bought 20%, and the three executives, who each purchased a £1m stake. The market capitalisation at the rights issue price of 125p was over £18m.

Most of the ingredients for a successful shell were in place: above all, three very able entrepreneurs with superb track records

and wonderful backing. The shares soared and several acquisitions were made, most of which were very successfully reorganised and rationalised afterwards. The share price of 180p (after a one for two scrip issue) in June 1992 is now well backed by earnings and compares with 125p for the rights in September 1988. A gain of 116% in just under four years — very good for a conventional industrial company but modest for a successful shell. The management, which is excellent (and will, I am sure, do very well in the future), did not put a foot wrong except for their very first one — starting with much too large a vehicle, at too heavy a price for a shell. Take my advice and avoid big shells. Stick to fleas — elephants don't gallop.

I much prefer low-priced shares. Companies often lose their shell-like quality as their share prices rise over £1. We all know that the price of a share makes no difference really and that owning four shares with a nominal value of 25p is the same as owning one share at £1. Nevertheless, when a share becomes 'heavier' and the price rises over £1, the press and brokers are more likely to have a serious look at the company and analyse the fundamentals. Shells thrive on future hope and a hint of mystery. Shells are about travelling, not arriving, so from the investment point of view arrival should be postponed as long as possible. My favourite price for a shell is between 5p and 10p. My second choice would be under 15p, then 20p and then 25p. The smaller and more like a flea the better.

A problem with shells priced at very low levels is the spread in the market, and that is one reason for not going below 5p. A 3p share, for example, would, probably, be priced at 2.75p-3.25p, giving the market makers a colossal turn of 0.5p — equivalent to 16.7%. In spite of this drawback, I prefer low-priced shares for a shell. An 8p share could easily rise to 10p in a few hours and 12p by the following day — that would be an increase of 50%. Very few shares of 80p could rise to 120p in the same 48 hours and certainly an £8 share would find it very hard going to reach £12 in six months, never mind a couple of days. For a shell, any price from 5p to 50p is highly attractive, as the first major psychological barrier of £1 is still some distance away. The moment of truth can sometimes be postponed, even with the shares trading at much higher levels of £2 to £3, but as the share price becomes heavier, so the share begins to lose one of the essential characteristics of a shell. At £3, they are in grave danger of someone deciding that they are a serious company and should be valued accordingly.

8. Avoid any shell unless it has a full listing or is on the USM. Bulletin Board quotations and shares that trade by matched bargains are not good enough for your purposes. Institutions avoid them like the plague and it is almost impossible to deal either way if you are in a hurry.

9. My last criterion is the liquidity of the company. Shells are obviously a much riskier kind of investment than leading companies. They find it more difficult to borrow in recessionary times — they are more likely to run out of money. Make sure that yours at least start off with a net cash balance or containable borrowings.

The high risk of investment in shells can be reduced by good portfolio management. Do not be fooled by remarks like '5p is only option money' and 'All you can lose is 5p.' If you have invested 5p and you lose 5p, you have lost all your money on that investment. It can happen very easily and must be expected more frequently with shells than with more established companies.

The first rule of shell portfolio management is to spread your investments over at least ten shares, preferably in equal amounts. A few more if you like, but never less than ten.

The second rule is to cut losses when shares drop by 40% from your cost. This may seem to be a very high limit but the market maker's turn can account for 10%-15% and shells are very narrow market, volatile stocks. You do not want to be taken out of your carefully selected investments by a minor and temporary blip. When your 40% limit is reached, simply cut your loss. The new managing director might have dropped dead or moved on to another company, or there could be some other major adverse development. Needless to say, when you know for certain that the story has changed for the worse, you should always sell immediately.

The third and most difficult rule is to run profits. Before we decide how far to run them, let us look at the arithmetic of the performance of a notional shell portfolio containing ten shares over a period of one year:

Company	Initial Investment (£)	Loss (%)	Gain (%)	Final Value (£)
A	1000	40	–	600
B	1000	–	60	1600
C	1000	–	30	1300
D	1000	40	–	600
E	1000	–	250	3500
F	1000	40	–	600
G	1000	–	150	2500
H	1000	60	–	400
I	1000	–	350	4500
J	1000	100	–	–
	£10,000			£15,600

With company H we missed selling at a 40% loss when the price of the shares dropped suddenly. Company J was suspended and was subsequently found to be insolvent, so we lost all of our money on this one. Companies E, G and I were the real winners — especially Company I.

With ten well-selected shares I would normally expect three big winners, four moderate winners and three losers. To be conservative, I assumed that we had five losers, one of which cost us more than might have been expected. On the plus side, I assumed that we had five winners, three of which had an average gain of 250%. We only enjoyed these large gains because we ran the profits. Most of the losses were contained because we cut them before they became more serious.

Our average gain over the year was 56% — a very worthwhile performance. Even if we had lost everything on the five losing shares, the average gain would still have been a satisfactory 34%. The credit for these above average gains must be attributed to the policy of running profits. There is no other explanation. Imagine the horrific performance if we had followed the much more natural policy of clinging to losses in the hope that the shares would recover, and snatching profits, nervously and prematurely, because we were frightened that they would disappear. We would almost certainly have lost money.

There is no easy guide for when to take a profit. Frequently, I add to my profit-makers when they have done well for me and are on all time highs, but you might find this very difficult psychologically. My simple suggestion to you is to allow your profits to run for a year, unless of course the story changes. The most important consideration is to let your little flea jump as high as it can. Give your flea a year to show how well it can perform. You will be very happily surprised sometimes.

After the year is up, check the fundamentals and assess each share for what it is really worth. What are the press, brokers and investment newsletters saying about the shares? Would you buy the shares now? What are the prospective earnings, the P/E ratio and the asset backing? Is there a large float of shares, and have any of the directors been selling? These are the kind of questions to ask yourself. If it has been a successful investment, the company is almost certainly no longer a shell, and should be reviewed like any other investment, strictly on its merits, in comparison with other shares in the same sector of the market.

Bear in mind that there is an extra advantage of running profits and cutting losses — you will keep your tax bill at a minimum. In a way, the Government is giving you an interest-free loan of the tax that will be due when your profits are realised. With shell investment, in particular, this can be a factor to take into account, but tax considerations should *never* over-ride a strong feeling that shares should be sold.

When in doubt, you can always sell half your holding in a big profit-maker. I do not like being half right and half wrong, but some people find this makes it easier to have the courage to run the residual profit. What are they so worried about anyway? Whether or not to take a very large profit is a great luxury to be enjoyed, so never agonise too much over the decision. Investing in fleas should be fun.

13

ASSET SITUATIONS AND VALUE INVESTING

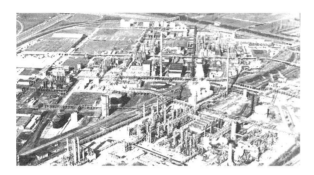

INVESTORS WHO CONCENTRATE UPON ASSET SITUATIONS ARE NOT SO INTERESTED IN IMMEDIATE EARNINGS. They reason that if a company holds the right kind of assets, earnings will flow from them eventually. If the existing management fails to deliver, new management or a predator will arrive on the scene to put the assets to work.

Determining the real asset value of a company is not an easy task, especially nowadays. At one time, you could rely upon substantial assets like major properties being understated in the balance sheet. In a very recessionary climate the reverse is often the case. In June 1992, Speyhawk has just announced a write-down of its assets of a massive £205m. The shares were 140p at their 1991 peak and were 2.5p after the news. Before the collapse, the shares were already trading at an 87% discount to their last published net asset value. Investors were obviously aware that the previous set of accounts were not to be relied upon.

How could this kind of over-valuation have occurred? There are a number of ways. Individual properties might have been valued based on the rents being received by other landlords of comparable buildings. However, in some cases there might have been substantial inducements to incoming tenants, such as a couple of years rent-free occupation and payment of the tenants' costs for fitting out offices. Meanwhile, the disadvantages of high gearing were becoming more apparent as property values tumbled during the year.

Another asset that is difficult to value is plant and machinery. On a going concern basis the valuation might be substantial, but if a factory is closed down and machinery has to be sold, the proceeds can be derisory, especially in a difficult trading climate. Even Warren Buffett had a few problems on this score, when he decided to close the New Bedford textiles plant that was one of his earliest acquisitions. The management was hoping for a good figure for the sale of the machinery, which had a book value of $866,000. They were due for a surprise — at a public auction the proceeds were only $163,000.

Brand names are difficult if not impossible to value. In some balance sheets they are included almost for nothing but in others they are valued at hundreds of millions of pounds. Most companies do not value brands in their balance sheets. The few that do usually have a specific reason — RHM, for example, was prompted by the threat of being taken over.

The recommended treatment of goodwill and intangibles on acquisition is that they be written off against reserves in the first year. However, accounting guidelines are due on this difficult subject shortly, and meanwhile, from the investor's viewpoint, the key is to be certain that the brand names you are examining are very strong in their own right and will continue to provide an independent earnings stream for the company in the future.

Goodwill is another thorny issue. I recommend writing it off when you calculate the net asset value of a company in which you are interested. At the very least your valuations will be consistent and understated.

There is a new accounting proposal, which attempts to make the balance sheet show current or market values rather than the present mix of historic and ad hoc re-valuations. At the moment, the rule for fixed assets, such as properties, is that they should not be included at values in excess of market price. However, we have already seen that valuers interpret market price in many different ways.

When investing in an asset situation, look for net assets to be at least 50% more than the present share price. Do your best to double-check that the net assets are accurately stated, but remember this is not an easy task.

There are also a number of further protective criteria, which have to be satisfied:

1. Total debt must not be more than 50% of net asset value.

2. There must be moderate earnings. Do not buy into substantial loss makers, however strong the asset position.

3. The basic business of the company must be reasonably attractive and there must be obvious scope for recovery. Avoid ship-builders for example.

A great additional inducement is to see executive directors buying some shares. Not a mandatory criterion, but an excellent pointer.

Companies of particular attraction to predators are those that have several disparate parts. The ideal is one with a substantial loss-maker that almost cancels out the other profit making activities of the group. A predator would not take long to find a buyer for the loss-maker, even if he had to almost give away the offending subsidiary. The resultant swing in profitability is often spectacular.

I am not over-keen on asset situations and prefer to concentrate upon growth stocks, shells and turnarounds. At Slater Walker, I could usually arrange for an asset situation to be activated. Nowadays, like other investors, I have a long and boring wait, whereas growth stocks and turnarounds usually give much more immediate satisfaction.

Ben Graham, who wrote *The Intelligent Investor*, is the American archdeacon of 'Value Investing', which is not to be confused with investing in asset situations. Graham's most famous investment formula is to buy shares at a price that represented not more than two-thirds of a company's net current assets *deducting all prior charges and giving no credit for any of the fixed assets of the company* such as property, plant and machinery, brand names and goodwill. In other words, buying the assets that are convertible into cash at a discount, with the rest of the business thrown in for nothing! Graham recommended selling when the share price advanced to a price equal to the net current assets less all prior charges. When the formula worked the gain would therefore be 50%. Between 1946 and 1976 Graham found that this method produced a compound annual rate of return in excess of 19%.

Many people believe that the term 'Value Investing' only refers to buying assets at a discount. In fact, Value Investing is broader than that — the essential concept is to look for values with a significant margin of safety relative to share prices.

Graham worked on several different approaches to investment, but buying value in one form or another was always his underlying principle. Before we examine his other ideas, it is important for you to realise that following the other systems I have outlined is also a form of Value Investing.

When you buy shares in a dynamic growth company on a low P/E ratio, with a consequently low PEG factor, you are buying growth prospects at a discount. You are obtaining better value for money than by buying the market as a whole. Similarly, when you invest in a turnaround just as the action starts or in a cyclical before the cycle turns up, you are buying into a company at a substantial discount to its full potential.

The market price of a share and the underlying value of that share are two very distinct animals. The 'value' is always subjective — what are the assets worth, always open to many different interpretations — what are the future earnings going to be, again very much a matter of opinion. That is why Graham concentrated his first system around net current assets, which could be converted into cash, the one asset that has an indisputable value. Graham believed that the market price would fluctuate without rhyme or reason around the real value, often for a considerable period of time, but in the end value would win through. In the long run share prices move in sympathy with earnings per share, dividends, cash flow and net assets. This is the essential back-cloth for understanding Graham's other approaches to investment.

Graham's second most well-known system was to buy shares which had an earnings yield (the reciprocal of the P/E ratio — for example a share on a P/E of 8 has an earnings yield of 12.5%) of not less than double the yield on a triple A bond. If the yield on such a bond was 10% that would mean buying shares on a multiple of only 5. In addition, Graham used an extra protective caveat insisting that the total debt of the company should not exceed its tangible net worth. Analysing the previous thirty years, Graham concluded that this method would also have produced a compound annual rate of return of 19% — far more than the market as a whole over the same period.

Graham's third approach was to buy shares with a dividend yield of not less than two-thirds of the triple A bond yield. Again he insisted that the companies in question should not owe more than they were worth. The compound annual rate of return was almost the same at 18.5%.

An important feature of Graham's method was that every qualifying stock had to be bought. Personal likes and dislikes were not allowed. In all three cases, Graham sold stocks either if they had risen 50% or a two year period had elapsed, whichever came first. He also sold if dividends were passed and, with earnings-based shares, if earnings declined to such an extent that the current market price was 50% higher than the hypothetical purchase price.

Graham was a most systematic and ingenious fellow who liked to buy assets at a discount and shares with a low P/E ratio. He then put a protective net under his selections with the safety criterion of limiting debt to tangible net worth. In my system for buying dynamic growth shares I am prepared to buy on a higher P/E ratio than Graham, but I link this with the estimated growth rate and find my value from a low PEG factor. I then erect a far more comprehensive safety net with my other criteria.

Warren Buffett was a disciple of Ben Graham, but modified his approach. It is important to understand that Graham gives no credit in his figures for intangibles like goodwill and brand names. In contrast, Buffett looks for shares that offer good general value and have a strong business franchise, preferably backed by very strong brand names. Essentially, Buffett is seeking a growth share to have and to hold. Graham was looking for immediate and obvious value to be sold as soon as the shares had risen by 50%. Buffett prefers to wait for a decade or so for a gain of a few thousand per cent.

The difficulty of operating Ben Graham's most famous system (the market price of a share being no more than two-thirds of net current assets, after deducting all prior charges and bringing in nothing for other assets) is that for long stretches of time very few, if any, shares measure up to that incredibly high standard. If Graham was alive today, he might argue that you should simply withdraw from the market for a few years until conditions arise which offer you the value for money that you are seeking. Graham may be right, but my problem is that I would get so bored waiting.

14

—

LEADING SHARES

MAJOR COMPANIES ARE NO DIFFERENT FROM SMALLER COMPANIES. You will not find any shells amongst them, but you will find plenty of growth stocks, cyclicals, turnarounds and asset situations. One advantage of dealing in leading stocks is that there is undoubtedly a greater degree of safety. Large stocks are more established, more a part of the fabric of society, and therefore less likely to fail from lack of funds or unexpected disasters. Furthermore, the market in the shares of larger companies is far more liquid. With a small company, you will quite often find that the market has suddenly contracted to only 1000 shares with a very wide spread. With leading shares, you should always be able to deal when you come to take your profits or cut your losses.

A disadvantage of leading shares is that they are usually more expensive as they have invariably been heavily researched. Overleaf, you will see two extracts from the June 1992 *Estimate Directory* — one for MTL Instruments and the other for GEC. Eighteen brokers have researched and written about GEC against only two who have bothered with MTL. The extensive coverage of GEC should give you a more reliable consensus forecast, but the over-exposure, coupled with the attractions of better marketability, tends to result in higher PEGs for blue chips.

A further disadvantage of leading shares is, of course, that elephants

THE MTL INSTRUMENTS GROUP PLC

Ordinary shares of 10p

Price 356p
Market cap. £63m

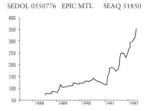

SEDOL 0550776 EPIC MTL SEAQ 51850

Activities The principal activity is the design, manufacture and marketing of electronic explosion-protection instruments and devices for use in the measurement and control of industrial processes carried out in hazardous environments. The group also manufactures electrical and surge-protection safety devices and gas analysis equipment. Manufacture takes place mainly in the UK and also in India for local distribution. Products are marketed in some 50 countries.

	Notes	Date of Forecast	12/92F PBT	EPS	DPS	12/93F PBT	EPS	DPS
BZW	B	5/3/92	5.1	18.5	3.85	5.7	20.6	4.30
Beeson Gregory	B	28/5/92	5.0	18.1	3.90	5.6	20.2	4.50
Consensus			5.1	18.3	3.88	5.7	20.4	4.40
% Change on Previous Year			+10	+10	+14	+12	+11	+14
Prospective P/E and DY on consensus				19.5	1.5		17.5	1.6

Year ended 12/91

PBT	4.6	P/E	21.4	
EPS	16.6	Dividend Yield	1.2	
Tax Charge	37			
Net Dividend	3.40			

Major Shareholders

I Hutcheon	10.37%
E Low	8.97%
L Towle	7.36%
T Barrett	6.96%
Hilary Menos	6.65%
J Burkitt	5.72%
C Burkitt	5.72%
C Oudar	5.70%

Price Relative

1m	+4%
3m	+13%
12m	+65%

Announcements

Interims	12/9/91
Finals	5/3/92
Report and Accounts	1/4/92
AGM	1/5/92

THE GENERAL ELECTRIC COMPANY PLC

Ordinary shares of 5p

Price 222p
Market cap. £5993m

SEDOL 0365334 EPIC GEC SEAQ 45337

Activities The manufacture of electronic, electrical and power generation apparatus and systems. The activities are divided into eleven divsions: electronic systems, power systems, telecommunications, consumer goods, electronic metrology, office equipment and printing, medical equipment, electronic components, industrial apparatus, distribution and trading and other activities.

	Notes	Date of Forecast	3/92F PBT	EPS	DPS	3/93F PBT	EPS	DPS
BZW	B	30/3/92	820.0	18.4	9.40	860.0	19.7	10.06
Charles Stanley	BI	13/1/92	840.0	18.8	9.50	900.0	20.0	10.00
County NatWest	H	24/4/92	815.0	18.4	9.30	845.0	19.4	9.70
Credit Lyonnais Laing	B	1/4/92	820.0	18.7	9.60	870.0	19.8	10.20
Girozentrale Gilbert Elliot	B	26/5/92	830.0	19.0	9.50	865.0	19.7	10.00
Hoare Govett	UV	22/4/92	810.0	18.3	9.25	835.0	19.0	9.25
James Capel	B3	27/4/92	820.0	18.4	9.50	865.0	19.7	10.00
Kleinwort Benson	B	24/3/92	840.0	18.7	9.50	920.0	20.9	10.30
Lehman Brothers	3M	20/5/92	835.0	19.1	9.25	917.0	21.0	9.90
Nikko	LTB	4/12/91	840.0	19.1	9.30	900.0	20.5	9.80
Nomura	H	28/5/92	815.0	18.6	9.40	855.0	19.9	9.80
Panmure Gordon	H/B	3/6/92	830.0	18.8	9.55	890.0	20.1	10.20
S.G.S.T. Securities	ADD	2/6/92	850.0	19.3	9.60	900.0	20.7	9.90
Salomon	B	23/4/92	830.0	18.6	9.25	870.0	19.8	10.00
Smith New Court	B	24/1/92	830.0	18.9	9.40	855.0	19.6	9.70
UBS Phillips & Drew	B	10/4/92	830.0	18.8	9.60	880.0	20.1	10.10
Warburg	ADD	7/4/92	820.0	18.6	9.50	860.0	19.6	9.90
Williams De Bröe	H	2/4/92	855.0	19.2	9.20	910.0	20.1	9.80
Consensus			829.1	18.8	9.43	877.0	20.0	9.93
% change on previous year			+1	+1	+2	+6	+6	+5
Prospective P/E and DY on consensus				11.8	5.7		11.1	6.0

Year ended 3/91

PBT	817.6	P/E	11.9	
EPS	18.6	Dividend Yield	5.5	
Tax Charge	35			
Net Dividend	9.25			

Major Shareholders

Prudential Corp. Group	7.04%
Phillips & Drew Fund Management	3.01%

Announcements

Interims	4/12/91
Finals	2/7/91
Report and Accounts	5/8/91
AGM	6/9/91

Price Relative

1m	-0%
3m	-1%
12m	+3%

don't gallop, although they do charge occasionally. If you intend to invest in them, you should be looking for one that is about to break away from the herd. You might well ask how you can tell. The answer is simple — apply exactly the same principles to investing in leading companies as you would to small companies. In PEG terms you will have to stretch your limit a little as you will find very few with a PEG of under 0.66, or for that matter 0.75. To keep the formula simple, I suggest a limit of one — the prospective multiple should not be more than the estimated growth rate.

As you know, I prefer growth shares with market capitalisations of under £100M. Most of the shares in the FT-A 500 Share Index are well over this figure. For the purposes of illustrating my approach to leading shares, I am, however, going to concentrate for the moment upon the FT-SE 100 Index in June 1992.

The formidable list shown overleaf needs to be broken down and analysed in detail. Let us first of all identify the super-growth shares — not from their reputation, but from their actual performance in recent years. A Datastream analysis can easily do this for us by applying a few selective criteria:

1. 15% compound growth in EPS over the last five years.

2. At least four years of positive growth.

3. EPS up at least 15% last year.

4. Dividends paid in each year and not cut at any time during the last five years.

Out of the 100 shares in the Index, there were only seven survivors — Rentokil, Rothmans, Sainsbury, Tate & Lyle, Tesco, Inchcape and Wellcome.

A few well-known growth shares are missing because the 15% EPS growth target is too harsh for the last recessionary year. If we drop the limit to 12% growth for that year only, one more share, Glaxo, scrapes through. If the limit for compound growth over the last five years is reduced to 12% per annum then four more shares make the grade — Argyll Group, Associated British Foods, British Telecom and Scottish & Newcastle. Reuters, with compound growth of 23%, and Guinness with 19.5% were unlucky to just fail at the last post, with 1991 EPS

FT-SE 100 INDEX ON 18TH JUNE 1992

Company	Latest year end	Growth in EPS					
		1987	1988	1989	1990	1991	1992
ABBEY NATIONAL	12/91	–	–	–	+16.7	+9.3	–
ALLIED-LYONS	2/92	+34	+17	+14	+4	+8	–
ANGLIAN WATER	3/91	–	–	–	–	+7	–
ARGYLL GROUP	3/92	+7	-1	+17	+25	+27	–
ARJO WIGGINS APL	12/91	–	–	–	–	-25	–
ASSD.BRIT.FOODS	9/91	+20	+2	+14	+21	+13	–
BAA	3/92	–	–	+30	+36	+21	–
BANK OF SCOTLAND	2/92	+21	+15	+29	+13	-44	-23
BARCLAYS	12/91	-71	+296	-54	-13	-39	–
BASS	9/91	+22	+12	+22	+9	-1	–
BAT INDS.	12/91	+1	+20	+21	-64	+34	–
BET	3/92	+19	+13	+16	+11	-35	–
BLUE CIRCLE IND.	12/91	+22	+19	+5	-23	-36	–
BOC GROUP	9/91	+39	+22	+11	+4	-15	–
BOOTS	3/92	+9	+7	+18	+20	-3	–
BOWATER	12/91	+34	+26	+26	-8	-2	–
BRIT. AEROSPACE	12/91	-100	–	-9	+63	-56	–
BRIT. PETROLEUM	12/91	+139	-20	+60	-1	-76	–
BRITISH AIRWAYS	3/91		+7	+22	+42	-43	–
BRITISH GAS	12/91	–	-3	+8	-4	+34	–
BRITISH STEEL	3/92	–	–	–	+1	-47	–
BRITISH TELECOM	3/92	+25	+10	+10	+10	+13	–
BTR	12/91	+11	+23	+27	-11	-10	–
CABLE & WIRELESS	3/92	+9	-5	+35	+20	-3	–
CADBURY SCHWEPPES	12/91	+30	+23	+8	+2	+7	–
CARLTON COMMS.	9/91	+35	+49	+34	-16	-33	–
COATS VIYELLA	12/91	+26	-41	-7	-20	-6	–
COMMERCIAL UNION	12/91	+7	+3	+9	-91	-100	–
COURTAULDS	3/92	+28	+6	-12	+16	+6	–
ENG.CHINA CLAYS	12/91	+22	+27	+5	-46	+24	–
ENTERPRISE OIL	12/91	+74	+5	+61	+14	-19	–
FISONS	12/91	+14	+21	+22	+18	-21	–
FORTE	1/92	+22	+16	–	–	+3	–
GENERAL ACCIDENT	12/91	+7	+25	-43	-100	–	–
GENERAL ELEC.	3/91	+5	+9	+14	+5	-7	–
GLAXO HDG.	6/91	+42	+15	+14	+21	+12	–
GRANADA GROUP	9/91	+21	+2	+23	-28	-47	–
GRAND MET.	9/91	+18	+24	+15	+16	+7	–
GT.UNVL.STORES	3/91	+24	+11	+4	+5	+4	–
GUARDIAN RYL.EX.	12/91	+6	+44	-41	-100	–	–
GUINNESS	12/91	+6	+25	+33	+24	+11	–
HANSON	9/91	+34	+11	+18	-2	-11	–
HILLSDOWN HDG.	12/91	+38	+22	+17	-19	-24	–
IMP.CHM.INDS.	12/91	+24	+13	-1	-33	-16	–
INCHCAPE	12/91	+48	+31	+6	-15	+21	–
KINGFISHER	1/92	+25	+9	+17	+11	+1	+0
LADBROKE GROUP	12/91	+28	+34	+24	+14	-40	–
LAND SECURITIES	3/92	+14	+11	+10	+16	+22	–
LASMO	12/90	–	-42	+176	+35	–	–
LEGAL & GENERAL	12/91	+6	+86	+3	-43	-44	–

FT-SE 100 INDEX CONTINUED

Company	Latest year end	Growth in EPS					
		1987	1988	1989	1990	1991	1992
LLOYDS BANK	12/91	-100	–	-100	–	+5	–
MARKS & SPENCER	3/92	+22	+19	+7	+12	+4	–
MB-CARADON	12/91	+30	+16	+12	-25	-4	–
NAT.WSTM.BANK	12/91	-39	+116	-71	-25	-41	–
NATIONAL POWER	3/92	–	–	–	–	–	–
NFC	9/91	–	–	–	+4	+7	–
NORTH WEST WATER	3/92	–	–	–	–	+207	–
NORTHERN FOODS	3/92	+13	+10	+10	+7	+16	–
PEARSON	12/91	+25	+7	+25	-13	-24	–
PEN.&ORNTL.DFD.	12/91	+11	+21	+21	-35	-22	–
PILKINGTON	3/92	+288	+7	+2	-7	-61	–
POWERGEN	3/92	–	–	–	–	–	–
PRUDENTIAL CORP.	12/91	+35	+31	+19	-53	+0	–
RANK ORG.	10/91	+25	+28	+2	-4	-41	–
RECKITT & COLMAN	12/91	+20	+23	+10	+12	+1	–
REDLAND	12/91	+29	+20	+38	-12	-41	–
REED INTL.	3/92	+18	+15	+1	+9	-16	–
RENTOKIL GROUP	12/91	+24	+38	+24	+21	+27	–
REUTERS HOLDINGS	12/91	+34	+23	+36	+14	+9	–
RMC GROUP	12/91	+38	+39	+17	-18	-36	–
ROLLS-ROYCE	12/91	–	+20	-0	-20	-51	–
ROTHMANS INTL.'B	3/92	+30	+16	+19	+23	+22	–
RYL.BK.OF SCTL.	9/91	-17	+132	-31	+5	-71	–
ROYAL IN.HDG.	12/91	-33	-15	-40	-100	–	–
RTZ CORP.	12/91	–	–	+18	-19	-25	–
SAINSBURY,J	3/92	+21	+23	+17	+24	+20	–
SCOT.& NEWCASTLE	4/91	+11	+11	+14	+20	+17	–
SCOTTISH POWER	3/92	–	–	–	–	–	–
SEARS	1/92	+12	+9	+12	-18	-27	–
SEVERN TRENT	3/91	–	–	–	–	+2	–
SHELL TRANSPORT	12/91	+13	+3	+46	-7	-43	–
SIEBE	3/91	+13	+36	+16	+15	-19	–
SMITH & NEPHEW	12/91	+14	+11	+11	-10	-7	–
SMITH,WH GP.'A'	5/91	+20	+18	+13	+10	-2	–
SMITHKLINE BHM.A	12/91	–	–	–	+14	+21	–
SUN ALL.GP.	12/91	–	–	-15	-100	–	–
TATE & LYLE	9/91	+35	+23	+29	+11	+16	–
TESCO	2/92	+40	+19	+13	+21	+27	+14
THAMES WATER	3/91	–	–	–	–	+24	–
THORN EMI	3/92	+50	+40	+17	+11	-19	–
TOMKINS	4/91	+71	+42	+35	+21	+0	–
TSB GROUP	10/91	+62	+45	+13	-34	-100	–
UNILEVER	12/91	+15	+3	+30	+8	+7	–
UNITED BISCUITS	12/91	+14	+15	+5	+2	+5	–
VODAFONE GP.	3/92	–	–	–	+91	+42	–
WELLCOME	8/91	+33	+38	+29	+18	+25	–
WHITBREAD'A'	2/92	+9	+14	+13	+18	+11	–
WILLIAMS HDG.	12/91	+31	+32	+10	-24	+1	–
WILLIS CORROON	12/91	-26	-37	+33	+17	-18	–

SOURCE : DATASTREAM

growth of 9% and 11% respectively. We will admit them, together with Vodafone and SmithKline Beecham, which had strong growth but short records.

Many well-known names failed to measure up to our criteria. For example, Marks and Spencer and Tomkins, because last year earnings were up only fractionally; and Hanson, as last year's earnings were down a little.

Our final list is only sixteen shares — about one in every six from the FT-SE 100 Index. Remember Chapter Seven on Competitive Advantage and notice the common characteristics of the sixteen shares. Five are in food retailing and manufacture, two are brewers and distillers and three are drug businesses with well-patented products. Rothmans has excellent international brand names and Rentokil has a very strong business franchise.

We will use the June 1992 *Estimate Directory* prices and future forecasts to see how the prospective PEGs of these fine companies measure up to our increased limit of one:

1. ARGYLL GROUP
Consensus forecast for the year ending 3/93 of EPS growth of 11%. Prospective P/E ratio at 350p equals 13.1, giving a PEG of 1.19.

2. GUINNESS
Consensus forecast for year to 12/92 of EPS growth of 11% and 13% in the following year. At 608p the average prospective P/E ratio for 1992/3 is 15.4 against average growth of 12%, giving a PEG of 1.28.

3. RENTOKIL
Consensus forecast of year to 12/92 of 21% growth and 19% in following year. Prospective P/E ratio for 1992 at 179p is 23.9 and 19.9 for 1993. The average prospective P/E for the year ahead is therefore 21.9 against average growth of 20%, giving a PEG of 1.10.

4. ROTHMANS
Consensus forecast growth for year to 3/93 of 9%. Prospective P/E ratio at 1100p about 11.9, giving a prospective PEG of 1.32.

5. SAINSBURY
Consensus forecast growth for year to 3/93 of 13%, giving a prospective P/E ratio of 16.6 at a price of 475p. The PEG is therefore 1.28.

6. TATE & LYLE
Consensus forecast for year to 9/92 of 1%, and for year to 9/93 of 10% — say 5.5% on average. At 392p, on a prospective P/E ratio of 11 with a very high PEG of 2.

7. TESCO
Consensus forecast for year to 2/93 of 9% growth with a prospective P/E ratio at 281p of 12.8, giving a prospective PEG of 1.42.

8. WELLCOME
Consensus forecast for year to 8/92 of a further 24% growth with 23% forecast for following year. Prospective P/E ratio at 971p of 21.8 for 1993, giving a prospective PEG of 0.94. A clear system buy.

9. GLAXO
Consensus forecast for 1993 of 15% growth with a prospective P/E ratio at 771p of 19.7, giving a prospective PEG of 1.31.

10. ASSOCIATED BRITISH FOODS
Negative forecast of minus 31% in EPS for year ending 9/92. Forget it.

11. BRITISH TELECOM
Fall in earnings forecast for year to 3/93. Forget it.

12. SCOTTISH & NEWCASTLE
Consensus 4/93 forecast of 9%, giving a prospective P/E ratio at 467p of 12.5 and a PEG of 1.39.

13. REUTERS
Consensus forecast for year to 12/92 of 11% growth and 13% for year to 12/93. Prospective P/E ratio at 1190p of 18.5, giving a PEG of 1.54, based on the average growth rate.

14. VODAFONE
Consensus forecast for year to 3/93 of 11% growth in EPS of a prospective P/E ratio at 383p of 19.1, giving a high prospective PEG of 1.74.

15. SMITHKLINE BEECHAM
Consensus forecast for 1992 of 13% growth and 15% for 1993. Average prospective P/E ratio at 924p of 15.8, giving a PEG of 1.13.

SMITHKLINE BEECHAM'S RIBENA

16. INCHCAPE

Consensus forecast for year to 12/92 of EPS growth of 17% and 14% in the following year. At 505p the average prospective P/E ratio for 1992/3 is 15 against average growth of 15.5%, giving a PEG of 0.97.

Most of the sixteen shares were fully priced. Let us look at the range of PEGs again:

0.94	Wellcome	Under 1.0
0.97	Inchcape	
1.10	Rentokil	
1.13	SmithKline Beecham	Between 1.00 and 1.20
1.19	Argyll Group	
1.28	Guinness	
1.28	Sainsbury	Between 1.20 and 1.35
1.31	Glaxo	
1.32	Rothmans	
1.39	Scottish & Newcastle	
1.42	Tesco	
1.54	Reuters	Over 1.35
1.74	Vodafone	
2.00	Tate & Lyle	
—	Associated British Foods	No longer applicable
—	and British Telecom	

We have only managed to find two shares, Wellcome and Inchcape, that appear to be bargains in terms of the price to be paid for future growth. One reason for Wellcome's inclusion is probably the proposed sale of £3bn worth of shares by the Wellcome Foundation. Some market makers might have depressed the price a little by selling shares, hoping to reload at a lower figure. By dropping our limit to a prospective PEG of 1.20 we expanded the portfolio to five shares. I was delighted to see that Rentokil was the first amongst them, as this has always been one of my favourite shares in the Index. By reducing the limit to 1.35, we admitted another four shares, giving a total of nine.

I am sure you will have noticed that the top nine selections, except Inchcape, have a strong competitive advantage and are in preferred industries. As you would expect their rate of return on capital employed is also startlingly above average.

Let us look at the details:

AVERAGE RATE OF RETURN ON CAPITAL EMPLOYED 1987-91

	%
Wellcome	26.53
Inchcape	26.29
Rentokil	53.34
SmithKline Beecham*	43.73
Argyll Group	26.67
Guinness	23.51
Sainsbury	22.60
Glaxo	37.12
Rothmans	26.48

*In the case of SmithKline Beecham the average rate of return is for only three years, 1989-91.

SOURCE : DATASTREAM

Before we continue, there are four important points to be made:

1. Prices, company results, forecasts and markets are constantly changing. I can only give you a snapshot of the position in June 1992.

2. The arithmetic used is very rough and ready, without examining in great detail company debt, interim results and the like. My intention is simply to explain the basic idea.

3. We are currently in a very deep recession, which is adversely affecting last year's results and next year's forecasts of many fine companies that would otherwise have been included. However, testing times like these separate the super-growth stocks from the herd.

4. The Datastream screening was designed to select consistent growth shares and undoubtedly will have missed many recovery situations and turnarounds that offer very good value for money.

The average estimated growth rate of the top nine shares is 14.8% next year, and the average prospective P/E ratio is about 17. The average prospective P/E ratio of the FT-SE 100 Index depends upon your view of the prospective growth rate. The historic P/E ratio for the FT-SE 100 Index was 16.5 in mid-June 1992 and I estimate (especially after Fisons' disappointing results and the June CBI review) that 5% is the *maximum* likely average growth rate for earnings next year. This view is currently shared by a number of leading brokers and if right will give a prospective P/E ratio for the index as a whole of about 15.7. You can readily see that to buy our top nine shares with proven records on an average prospective P/E ratio of 17, budgeting for a much more reliable 14.8% average earnings growth in the year ahead, is an obvious bargain when compared with buying the average FT-SE 100 share on a prospective 15.7 multiple, budgeting for much lower and *much less reliable* growth of only 5% in 1992/3. In other words, there is a negligible premium for established super-growth.

I was so surprised to reach this conclusion that I double-checked the FT-SE 100 Index to eliminate the large number of finance companies and recovery situations on very high multiples and the utilities on very low ones. The final result was the same — the super-growth shares still seem to be a *relative* bargain. In spite of this, the prices of our nine shares seem very expensive to me. This is almost certainly due to the market, in June 1992, being within 10% of its all-time high whereas the economic outlook remains bleak. If you deal in the top one hundred stocks, you need to become used to paying up for much higher PEGs in exchange for better marketability and extra security. With *patient* money I would much prefer to buy shares in smaller companies with PEGs of under 0.66. There will be times when you cannot deal, but provided the money invested is not needed for other purposes, the risk/reward ratio of investing in smaller companies with much lower PEGs seems to me to be a better proposition.

The first one hundred shares in the index are rather special, so let us analyse the second hundred (Tootsie) in a similar way to see if we can find any attractive bargains. The only shares that qualify with a 15% five year compound growth rate and with growth of 15% last year are Iceland Frozen Foods, Dunhill, W. Morrison, Spring Ram, Kwik-Save and The Body Shop. Iceland has a prospective PEG of 0.85, Spring Ram of 0.87 and The Body Shop of 0.90. All three companies enjoy a very high rate of return on capital employed.

I have only analysed the first two hundred shares from the

ICELAND STORE

perspective of seeking out growth shares that are relatively attractive. Needless to say, there is also a large number of turnarounds, cyclicals and asset situations in the Index. An excellent example of a recent turnaround now in the FT-SE 100 Index is English China Clays, which I have already mentioned in Chapter Eleven. Another less well-known example in the first five hundred shares is Amersham International, which caught my eye a month or so before the results were announced in June 1992. At 483p, the price after the announcement of earnings per share up a dazzling 44%, the market capitalisation was about £250m. The company's activities include life science research, health care and industrial quality and safety assurance. Amersham has only a trivial £700,000 of debt and the brokers' consensus forecast for 1992/3 was profits before tax of £24.7m to give growth of 20% next year. However, the brokers' forecasts were made before the better than expected results, and I noticed in the *Evening Standard* that one broker was already considering upgrading its 1992/3 forecast to £26.5m before tax, putting the shares on a prospective multiple of 16.5. The growth from £20.7m to £26.5m is £5.8m which would be 28%. To be conservative, let us say 25%, giving a PEG of 0.66 (25 divided into 16.5), just qualifying for my system for small companies.

Amersham International, a wonder stock of the eighties, is making a recovery from a period of four years of declining profits as a result of the more cost-conscious and commercial approach of a new management team headed by Bill Castell. Some of the earnings growth may therefore come from one-off improvements, but, nevertheless, the shares seem to me to be attractive for a business of this size and quality.

The further down the scale you are prepared to invest, the better the bargains in terms of the prospective PEG. Amongst the top one hundred shares we could only find two shares that fulfilled our criteria and had a prospective PEG of under one. In the second hundred, we found three shares with more attractive PEGs. Further down the scale, we identified Amersham International as a bargain on a prospective PEG of 0.66. Moving on further into the second thousand shares, you can find companies like British Data Management on a prospective PEG of 0.45 and Industrial Control Services on 0.60. In some ways, you can compare the spectrum of differing PEGs with bargain hunting for antiques — if you buy an antique table in a Bond Street shop you have to pay a price that makes a contribution to their London High Street rental. However, if the collector's item you purchased had a major fault, you would be more likely to be able to get your money back from the Bond Street

BILL CASTELL

shop than from a small, out-of-the-way antique shop in a side street near Euston Station. The shares in smaller companies are undoubtedly riskier and less marketable, and that is reflected in the PEG you pay. My argument is that frequently the bargain value becomes irresistible.

If you are interested in recovery stocks you should read the book by Michael O'Higgins — *Beating the Dow*. His basic system is to take the ten highest yielding Dow thirty share stocks at the beginning of each year and then select the five with the lowest dollar prices. (He observes that lower priced stocks usually have smaller market capitalisations and that smaller companies tend to register greater percentage gains than larger ones. He does not go on to say that elephants don't gallop but we know where he is coming from). O'Higgins argues that by following his simple system over the last twenty years, you would have enjoyed an average annual rate of return of over 20%, compared with 10.92% on the Dow. Philip Coggan ran a similar test on UK stocks in the *Financial Times*, and found that, since 1979, £10,000 *with dividends reinvested* would have grown into more than £130,000 by early 1992. The same sum invested in the FT-A All-Share Index, also with dividends reinvested, would have grown to £81,540. The qualification of dividends being reinvested is an important one, as the shares selected under the system are high yielding.

If you decide that you want to concentrate your investments in larger companies, I recommend that you confine your activity to the top five hundred shares. The next step would be to determine your investment criteria for the kind of share you are trying to identify. For example, with asset situations, a discount to book value without excessive debt or current losses; for cyclicals, sales of over five times market capitalisation, asset backing of 80% or more of the share price and gearing not in excess of 100% of net asset value. You should then arrange, with your by-now-startled broker, for a Datastream analysis. When you have a small list of shares that have successfully run the gauntlet, you should read the press cuttings and study the annual reports and *The Estimate Directory* forecasts for the companies in question, to make sure that your other safety criteria are all in place.

You will find this approach much better than buying a share just because it takes your fancy. There could easily be a gem hidden amongst the five hundred top shares, and the one thing you know for certain is that you are unlikely to find something hidden without a search.

15

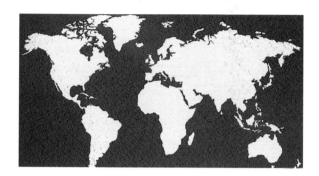

OVERSEAS MARKETS

MY SYSTEM FOR INVESTMENT IN DYNAMIC GROWTH STOCKS WORKS EXCEPTIONALLY WELL FOR AMERICAN SHARES AND WILL ALSO WORK WELL IN MANY OTHER OVERSEAS MARKETS. The important differences between America and the UK are that American accounting standards are far higher, results are quarterly, there are more growth companies and the degree of sophistication in investment management is in a different dimension.

Before you begin to invest in America, your reading habits will have to be expanded. *The Wall Street Journal*, a wonderful newspaper on a par with the *Financial Times*, is a daily must. *Value Line*, a truly exceptional weekly publication that would be hugely successful in the UK, is also mandatory. Each week about 200 companies are analysed in depth and rated by a *Value Line* analyst as to Timeliness and Safety. Very detailed statistics are given for each share showing quarterly earnings growth, balance sheets, book value, a chart of the share price, relative strength and an analyst's detailed review. *Value Line's* top recommendations for Timeliness have substantially out-performed the market year after year.

In addition to reviews on individual shares, *Value Line* has further statistics on all the shares under review, highlighting high yielding stocks, high cash flow generators, widest discounts from book value, lowest P/E ratios, highest percentage returns on capital and high growth stocks. Paradise for the investment analyst.

A few years ago, I remember finding Celanese shares at $68 amongst the list of those at a discount to asset value and amongst the shares on a particularly low P/E ratio. Celanese also had $28 per share in cash. A real gem — a year or so later the company was taken over for $245 per share by Hoechst of Germany.

Barron's is a fine weekly paper that is broadly the equivalent of the *Investors Chronicle*, albeit that *Barron's* is written in a racier style with a much more overt sense of humour. In addition to guiding you on your American investments, *Barron's* will also help to give you a far better global perspective. Another important contribution to this end is *The Bank Credit Analyst* from Toronto, a superb monthly publication giving detailed statistics and views on the trend of world markets and currencies, with particular reference to Wall Street and the dollar.

Armed with my system, you can easily work from *Value Line's* weekly reviews. You should ignore what their analysts say about Timeliness and Safety and simply calculate the PEG factor yourself and apply my other criteria. Once you have reached your own conclusions, double check your final view with the *Value Line* rating. You will be surprised how often your selections will be rated highly for Timeliness. If the *Value Line* Safety rating is very low be on guard and double check your figures. You will probably find that the borrowings are very high or there is some other major problem. Always remember that you do not have to invest. You can wait until the following week or month and continue your search for an absolute gem. Never invest for the sake of it.

Needless to say, you will need a broker who is well versed in American shares. Your English broker may well be able to handle purchases and sales for you, but you must ensure that you also receive some kind of feedback and are kept abreast of major developments. Although you cannot expect too much help, you must try to avoid dealing with a Post Office. You will need some guidance. For example, when checking the value of a share you must pay careful attention to three peculiarities of the American market:

1. POST-RETIREMENT MEDICAL LIABILITIES

In days gone by, American managements, when negotiating with the unions, could be very generous with shareholders' funds by increasing post-retirement medical benefits for their employees and themselves.

Prior to 1992, you would have found no trace in the accounts of the liabilities arising from these benefits. Now, they have to be charged against profits. To catch up with the past, some major companies will be writing off billions in their next set of accounts.

2. PENSION FUND DEFICITS

As a result of new regulations, from now on Pension Fund deficits have to be written off against profits over a period of years. For some companies the charge could be massive.

3. ENVIRONMENTAL PROTECTION AGENCY

In the USA, there has been a considerable reaction against businesses causing environmental damage. Recently, new legislation was passed, and the Environmental Protection Agency was formed to set standards and apply the new regulations. Anybody who has suffered a loss as a result of previous environmental damage can sue the company that caused the damage and even go beyond the corporate veil to attack shareholders. As members of Lloyds will know, American juries tend to be anti-business and are awarding vast sums in damages.

The cumulative effect of these three relatively recent developments means that many American companies, thought to be in good shape, have very substantial potential financial liabilities hanging over them, which could in some instances affect their future viability.

Emerging markets such as Indonesia, Thailand and Mexico are often shunned by investors because of illiquidity, very high volatility and the currency risk. It is worth noting that even on a risk-adjusted basis, emerging markets have substantially out-performed both the USA and Europe. One reason is that the growth in Gross Domestic Product of developing countries is much faster than more mature economies like the USA, Germany, Japan and the UK. A high growth rate in GDP is a wonderful back-cloth for investment in an economy, usually leading to higher earnings for individual companies. Another reason for the better performance of emerging market shares is that they tend to be under-researched by the investment community, in the same way that smaller companies are sometimes neglected in mature markets. Each market has to be examined on its merits, with particular reference to political stability, the economic background, fundamental values, currency risk and the investment opportunities that are available.

Dr. Marc Faber in *The Gloom, Boom and Doom Report* gives a very interesting summary of the Life Cycle of Emerging Markets. As he says, 'First, stocks are in an embryonic stage. Then, when they reach adolescence, they grow very rapidly (bullish phase). During this stage, they are accident-prone (crashes). Later, markets mature, lose some of their energy and volatility, then become tired and finally die (bear markets)... Fortunately for stock markets, there is usually life after death. A new cycle begins which, like life after reincarnation, is very different in nature from the previous cycle.'

His six phases are depicted in the following graph.

THE LIFE CYCLE OF EMERGING MARKETS

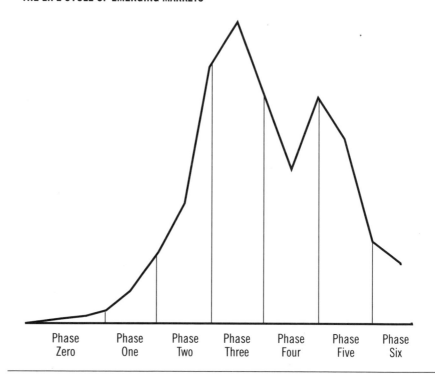

| Phase | Phase | Phase | Phase | Phase | Phase | Phase |
| Zero | One | Two | Three | Four | Five | Six |

Now let us look at what he says about each of the phases. His thoughts are well worth reading because they also give an excellent insight into the bull and bear cycle of all markets, which essentially move from no interest in stocks to a kind of mania, before going back to a phase in which investors give up on stocks again. Dr. Faber summarises his fascinating survey by making it clear that the objective

PHASE ZERO

EVENTS
- Long-lasting economic stagnation or slow contraction in real terms.
- Real per capita incomes are flat or have been falling for some years.
- Little capital spending, and international competitive position is deteriorating.
- Unstable political and social conditions (strikes, high inflation, continuous devaluations, terrorism, border conflicts, etc.)
- Corporate profits are depressed.
- No foreign direct or portfolio investments.
- Capital flight.

SYMPTOMS
- Little tourism (unsafe).
- Hotel occupancy is only 30%, and no new hotels have been built for several years. Hotels are run-down.
- Curfews at night.
- Little volume on the stock exchange.
- Stockmarket has been moving sideways or moderately down for several years.
- In real terms, stocks have become ridiculously under-valued.
- No foreign fund managers visit the country.
- Headlines in the press are negative. No foreign brokers have established an office, no country funds are launched, and no brokerage research reports have been published for a long time.

EXAMPLES
- Argentina in the eighties.
- Middle East prior to the seventies.
- Communist countries after World War II until recently.
- Sri Lanka prior to 1990.
- Philippines between 1980 and 1985.

PHASE ONE

EVENTS
- The social, political, and economic conditions begin to improve (new government, new economic policies, external factors, discoveries, the rise in price of an important commodity).
- Improvement in liquidity because of an increase in exports, the repatriation of capital, and increasing foreign direct and indirect investments.
- The outlook for future profit opportunities improves significantly.
- Increase in cash balances and wealth.
- Consumption, capital spending, corporate profits and stocks begin to rise sharply.

SYMPTOMS
- Stocks suddenly begin to pick up.
- Tourism improves.
- Foreign businessmen become interested in joint ventures and other direct investments.
- Hotel occupancy rises to 70%.
- A few foreign fund managers begin to invest.
- Curfews are lifted.
- Tax laws are changed to encourage capital formation and to attract foreign investors.

EXAMPLES
- Argentina after 1990.
- Thailand after 1985.
- Middle East after 1973.
- Mexico after 1984.
- China after 1978.
- Indonesia after 1988.

PHASE TWO

EVENTS
- Unemployment falls and wages rise.
- Capital spending in order to expand capacity soars, as the improvement in economic conditions is perceived to last forever (error of optimism).
- Large inflows of foreign funds propel stocks to overvaluation.
- Credit expands rapidly, leading to a sharp rise in real and financial assets.
- Real estate prices rise several fold.
- New issues of stocks and bonds reach peak levels.
- Inflation accelerates and interest rates begin to rise.

SYMPTOMS
- The business capital resembles an enormous construction site.
- Hotels are full of foreign businessmen and portfolio managers. Many new hotels are under construction.
- Headlines in the international press are now very positive.
- An avalanche of thick, bullish country research reports are published by foreign brokers. Foreign brokerage offices are opened up. Country funds are launched.
- The thicker the reports, the more offices that have opened up, and the more funds that are launched, the later it is within phase two.
- Countries in phase two tend to become favourite travel destinations.

EXAMPLES
- Thailand between 1987 and 1990.
- Japan between 1987 and 1990.
- Kuwait between 1978 and 1980.

PHASE THREE

EVENTS
- Overinvestments lead to excess capacity in several sectors of the economy.
- Infrastructural problems and an excessive credit expansion lead, via rising wages and real estate prices, to strong inflationary pressures.
- The rate of corporate profit growth slows down, and in some industries corporate profits begin to fall.
- A shock (a sharp rise in interest rates, a massive fraud, a business failure, or some external shock) leads to a sudden and totally unexpected decline in stock prices.

SYMPTOMS
- Many condominium and housing projects, and new hotels, office buildings, and shopping centres are completed.
- The business capital resembles a "boom town" – lively nightlife and heavy traffic congestion.
- Frequently a new airport is inaugurated and a second one is in the planning stages.
- "New cities" are planned and developed.
- Real estate and stockmarket speculators flourish, make the headlines with their rags-to-riches tales, and fill the nightclubs.
- The stock and real estate markets become a topic of discussion. There is active retail and speculative activity, much of it on borrowed money.
- The locals begin to invest actively overseas in things they have no understanding of (art, real estate, stocks, golf courses, etc).

EXAMPLES
- Thailand after 1990.
- Singapore in 1980 and 1981.
- Japan in 1990.
- Indonesia in 1990.

PHASE FOUR

EVENTS
- Credit growth slows down.
- Corporate profits deteriorate.
- Excess capacity becomes a problem in a few industries, but overall the economy continues to do well and the slowdown is perceived to be only temporary.
- After an initial sharp fall, stocks recover as foreign investors who missed the stockmarket's rise in phases one and two pour money into the market and as interest rates begin to fall.
- Stocks fail to reach a new high because a large number of new issues meet demand (the sellers are locals who know better or are strapped for cash).

SYMPTOMS
- Condominiums have reached prices which exceed the purchasing power of the locals. They are now advertised overseas.
- Office capital values and rentals begin to level off or fall.
- Tourist arrivals slow down and are below expectations. Hotel vacancy rates rise and discounts are offered.
- Brokers continue to publish bullish reports.
- Political and social conditions deteriorate (a coup, a strong opposition leader, strikes, social discontent, increase in crime, etc).

EXAMPLES
- Japan in the first half of 1991.
- Thailand in 1991.
- US investors in early 1930 and in the fall of 1973.

PHASE FIVE

EVENTS
- Credit deflation.
- Economic, but even more so social and political, conditions now deteriorate badly.
- Consumption slows down noticeably or falls (car sales, and housing and appliance sales are down).
- Corporate profits collapse.
- Stocks enter a prolonged and severe downtrend as foreigners begin to exit the market.
- Real estate prices fall sharply.
- A "big player" goes bankrupt (one who made the headlines in phase three).
- Companies are strapped for cash.

SYMPTOMS
- Empty office buildings, high vacancy in hotels, discontinued and unfinished construction sites are now common.
- Stockbrokers lay off staff or close down.
- Research reports become thinner. Country funds which sold at a premium during phases two and three now sell at a discount.
- The country is no longer a favourite tourist destination.

EXAMPLES
- Thailand in 1992.
- Singapore in 1982 and 1983.
- United States in 1931 and in late 1973.
- Japan in early 1992.

PHASE SIX

EVENTS

- Investors give up on stocks. Volume is down significantly from the peak levels reached in phase three.
- Capital spending falls (error of pessimism).
- Interest rates decline further.
- Foreign investors lose their appetite for any new investments.
- The currency is weakening or is devalued.

SYMPTOMS

- Headlines turn very negative.
- Foreign brokers finally turn bearish.
- Flights, hotels and nightclubs are empty.
- Taxi drivers, shopkeepers, and nightclub hostesses tell you how much they have lost by investing in stocks.

EXAMPLES

- United States in 1932 and at the end of 1974.
- Hong Kong in 1974.
- Japan??
- Thailand??
- Indonesia??

is of course to enter the emerging market in question in Phase Zero or Phase One. He points out that during Phases One and Two, an individual stock can easily rise twenty to fifty times in value. In the next phase you enter a high risk zone.

The Fountain of Wealth shown in Dr. Faber's newsletter attempts to categorise emerging markets according to their level of economic development and prosperity in June 1992. The analogy of a fountain is excellent, as water flows down from a higher level just as money flows down from rich countries with high price levels to poor countries with low price levels. The countries at the bottom of the fountain are still in Phase Zero but could move into Phase One at any time, provided the economic and legal infrastructure needed to attract foreign direct investors is put in place.

Countries like Argentina can move very quickly from one phase to another. Eighteen months ago Argentina might have been below the fountain, six months ago in the first water basin and in June 1992 in a higher basin still. Dr. Faber argues that today there are very few emerging countries with established stockmarkets which are still in Phase One. A few, like Brazil, Colombia and Argentina, might still be in Phase Two, but as they approach Phase Three the risk of a crash increases. Many countries have already reached Phase Four or Five; there is no rush to get back into them.

There is a great deal of money to be made by investing in an emerging market at precisely the right time, and remember that your choice of country can be more important than your choice of share. *The Bank Credit Analyst* has a new service, *Emerging Markets Analyst*,

THE FOUNTAIN OF WEALTH

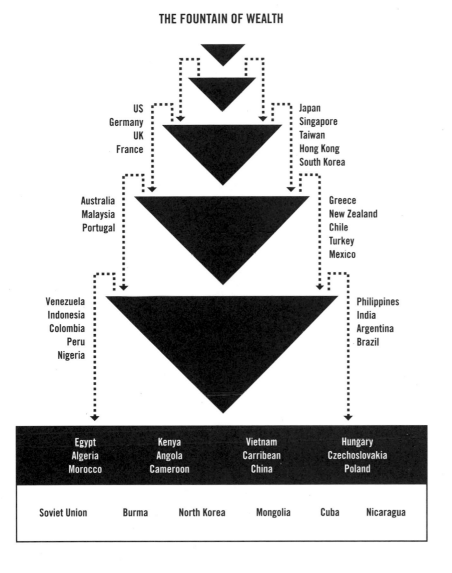

which should help you to make the right selection, and Marc Faber's newsletter also highlights attractive opportunities from time to time. However, as a potential follower of The Zulu Principle, you would probably be better advised to first become expert on one method of investment in your own back yard.

16

—

YOUR BROKER AND YOU

YOU MUST FIND A GOOD STOCKBROKER TO HELP YOU WITH YOUR INVESTMENTS. Most of the larger brokers naturally concentrate their efforts upon servicing the institutions, investment trusts, unit trusts and other major investors. Some brokers will not take on small private accounts unless the initial portfolio totals £100,000 or more. However, there are others who do not have a minimum limit and would be pleased to help private investors with a starting portfolio of as little as £10,000. Bernard Gray, in the *Beginners' Guide to Investment*, gives a list of private client brokers in Appendix C, together with their telephone numbers. Another source is the *Directory of Private Client Stockbrokers*, which is available free of charge from ProShare (Tel 071 600 0984).

Brokers' commission on purchases and sales of stock can range from 1.65% to less than 0.5% according to the size of the transaction and the importance of the client. You should not begrudge your broker a top of the range commission on each transaction, provided he gives you good service. You want a broker who is switched on and really anxious to help you. Quality of service is far more important than the rate of commission.

You have to bear in mind that your broker would be unnatural if he was not to some extent commission orientated. The more you turn over your portfolio, the more commission your broker will earn in the short run. However, I hasten to reassure you that most brokers have the long-term interests of their clients at heart and will not try to persuade them to deal simply to earn a commission. You should try to find a broker who is value-minded, not quotation-minded.

You also have to be on guard against brokers who have a favourite share that they keep tipping. Let me tell you the story of an American broker we will name Dan. He was very keen on the shares of a small company, Widgets Inc., which was quoted on NASDAQ in a very narrow market. He recommended a new client to buy 5000 for $2 each. The shares duly doubled in price. When the client telephoned to sell, Dan replied, 'You must be mad. The company has a new product that is far better than the original widgets and it has just signed a royalty agreement with a leading manufacturer. You should buy some more.' The client obliged and bought 2500 more shares for $4 each.

Within a few weeks, the shares had doubled again. 'Thanks a lot,' said the client. 'You've made me a great deal of money. Please sell all my shares now.'

'You must be mad,' said Dan. 'You know that manufacturer I told you about, it's going to take over Widgets. There should be an announcement during the next couple of weeks. I would buy some more.'

'Buy me another 1000,' replied the client.

A few weeks later, although there was no takeover, the shares had reached $16 each. The ecstatic client phoned his broker. Before Dan could say a word, he gave his instructions. 'I want you to sell all my shares now,' he said.

'To whom?' replied Dan.

The problem for many small investors is that they feel their initial account is so tiny and unimportant to the broker, that they cannot be too demanding. This is of course true, but there is an absolute minimum of information that the private investor, however small, can and should request. As the account grows there is another, higher level of service that can be progressively demanded. Let me outline for you the minimum standard you can reasonably expect as a small private investor:

1. Any verbal or written recommendation from your broker should be accompanied by details of the current P/E ratio of the share in

question, the dividend yield, the NAV per share, the market capitalisation, the past record of earnings growth, the brokers' consensus of estimated future growth, the prospective P/E ratio, borrowings and your broker's reasons for buying. A copy of the *Extel* card should also be available on request, together with information on the share's relative strength and details of any recent Directors' share dealings.

2. Any execution should be carried out efficiently, at the price limit mutually agreed with the broker.

3. Subsequently, you should be kept informed of any major new developments, such as Directors' share dealings, any announcements made by the company and details of any very sharp price movements.

As your relationship develops and you become a major client, you should expect your broker to provide a copy of the Datastream relative strength chart for any share in which you are interested, and if necessary obtain a copy of the annual and interim accounts for you. Also, your broker should be able to supply the last six months' press cuttings and a copy of any recent circulars by other major brokers. You cannot expect this kind of service until you are paying your broker sufficient commissions to justify special treatment. You should restrict your requests for the fullest information to those companies in which you are very likely to invest. Obviously you do not want to wear your broker's patience too thin with hundreds of spurious enquiries.

I have in the past dealt with brokers who ring me up to say, 'English China Clays looks very good. There is a rumour that Hanson are going to bid.' Or 'Tesco's results are coming out on Wednesday. They will be better than expected. The shares look very cheap.' I hate these kind of share tips. They are worse than useless — they are a definite drawback to good money management. When brokers tell me a share looks good, I immediately ask for details of the price earnings ratio, the asset value, the record over the last five years, the growth rate and the brokers' consensus forecast. I want facts and try to limit fancy. If you do the same, your broker will quickly get the message that you are one of those strange people who actually wants to concentrate upon the known facts first, second and last. Once you have established a modus vivendi with your broker, he or she can and should become an invaluable ally and aid to the successful management of your investments. It is important to start off as you mean to continue.

Your other aid to investment is your daily, weekly and monthly reading. You should not underestimate the importance of technical and trade magazines in the areas in which you specialise or have an interest. On occasions, you might notice a new brand or a new invention that is selling particularly well, and be in a position to take advantage of this information well before the general market. For financial news the bare minimum you require is the *Financial Times* every day, another good daily paper, a leading Sunday paper and the *Investors Chronicle* every week. The *Financial Times* is one of the finest newspapers in the world and an absolutely indispensable investment tool for investing in the UK stockmarket. Even if you do not have time to read the FT thoroughly every day, be sure to read the weekend edition, which summarises the week's movements in major markets and contains many excellent articles of a more general nature.

I take several daily papers and read most of the Sundays. In addition I subscribe to the *Fleet Street Letter*, which is published fortnightly, and to *The Investors Stockmarket Letter*, which is weekly. I also take *The Penny Share Guide* and *Penny Share Focus*, which are monthly publications concentrating upon smaller companies. *The Economist*, which is published weekly, is an excellent magazine for keeping in touch with world economic and financial developments. I particularly recommend to you the last couple of pages, which highlight Economic and Financial Indicators, showing the performance of world stockmarkets, money supply statistics, world interest rates, trade balances, reserves, exchange rates, industrial production, GNP, GDP, retail sales, unemployment, consumer and wholesale price movements and wage increases on a week by week basis.

During the last two years, I have also subscribed to *Analyst*, which has many interesting in-depth articles each month on investment systems and approaches as well as excellent company profiles and very detailed commentaries on smaller growth companies.

In the chapter on American shares, I mention *The Wall Street Journal*, *Barron's* and *The Bank Credit Analyst*, all of which help to give a global picture of the investment scene. In particular, I have found *The Bank Credit Analyst* excellent at determining major market trends, especially on Wall Street. *Value Line* is also an indispensable tool for investing in American shares.

I find extensive reading is essential to keep in tune with markets. To this end, another interesting newsletter is *The Gloom, Boom and Doom Report* which is edited by Dr. Marc Faber. He is often extremely bearish, which helps to cool me down when I begin to feel uppity.

I also subscribe to *The Estimate Directory*, which gives brokers' consensus estimates of future earnings and details of the brokers who have written circulars on the companies in question. There are also publications like *Directus*, which highlight Directors' share dealings, but, unless you transact a large volume of investment business yourself, you should be able to obtain these details through your broker, at least as far as they affect the shares in which you are particularly interested.

Before leaving the subject of reading about investment, I would like to recommend to you ten excellent American books which have influenced my investment thinking:

1. *The Intelligent Investor* by Benjamin Graham (Harper and Row USA). An investment classic which Warren Buffett believes is the 'best book on investing ever written.' The main subjects are the virtues of 'value investing' and a systematic approach. Not a quick and easy read, but full of revelationary and intriguing ideas.

2. *Security Analysis* by Graham and Dodd (McGraw-Hill Book Co. USA). The fifth edition brings this investment classic up to date. The book, which is very hard going, outlines in great detail the principles and techniques for measuring asset values, cash flow and earnings.

3. *Extraordinary Popular Delusions and the Madness of Crowds* by Charles Mackay (Farrar Strauss and Giroux USA). First published in 1841 — a classic on crowd psychology. Fun to read and one of my favourites.

4. *The Midas Touch* by John Train (Harper and Row USA). A detailed exposition on the strategies that have made Warren Buffett America's pre-eminent investor. An easy and entertaining read.

5. *Market Wizards* by Jack Schwager (Simon and Schuster Inc. USA). Interviews with top traders in commodities and stockmarkets, concentrating upon their individual approaches and attitudes.

6. *One Up on Wall Street* by Peter Lynch (Penguin). An excellent and very readable book by one of America's most successful mutual fund managers.

7. *Technical Analysis of Stock Trends* by Robert Edwards and John Magee (John Magee Inc USA). An authoritative book on technical analysis, but a very hard read. Only for the dedicated.

8. *The New Money Masters* by John Train (Harper and Row USA). A very readable account of the highly successful investment strategies of investment giants like Soros, Lynch and Rogers. Train's previous book, *The Money Masters*, is also good value.

9. *Reminiscences of a Stock Market Operator* by Edwin Lefevre (Fraser Publishing Company USA). An amusing account of Jessie Livermore's early life, showing how important it is not to fight the market but to go with the force.

10. *Beating the Dow* by Michael O'Higgins and John Downes (Harper-Collins USA). A detailed exposition on Dow stocks and a method of buying those that are out of favour to produce returns that dwarf the market averages.

To obtain copies of some of these books is often difficult. I suggest that you begin by enquiring at a leading book store like W.H.Smith, Hatchards or Foyles, but if unsuccessful you should try a specialist in books on business and investment such as The Business Bookshop, 72 Park Road, London NW1 4SH (Tel 071 723 3902) or Books Etc., 30 Broadgate, London EC2 (Tel 071 628 8944).

If you are not full time in the investment business, you might find some of the recommended books very hard going. I suggest, therefore, that you begin with those that are an easy read and entertaining as well as instructive. To get you in the mood, try first *One Up on Wall Street*, followed by *The Midas Touch* and *Beating the Dow*. If you are going to apply The Zulu Principle and master the subject of investment, there is no escape from further homework.

17

PORTFOLIO MANAGEMENT

A PRIVATE INVESTOR WITH A RELATIVELY SMALL PORTFOLIO HAS A CONSIDERABLE ADVANTAGE OVER INSTITUTIONS WITH MASSIVE FUNDS TO INVEST. The institutions have to spread their investments over as many as two hundred stocks, and in some cases even more. The private investor probably holds a maximum of ten to twelve shares in his portfolio. I work on twelve to fifteen, but on occasions as few as eight.

Why is investing in ten stocks an advantage over investing in a hundred? Your first choice is obviously far better than your tenth, which in turn should be considerably better than your hundredth. Secondly, the fewer stocks in your portfolio, the easier it is for you to keep a really keen eye on them all. The Zulu Principle again.

After my initial due diligence, I always try to keep a watching brief over the few stocks that constitute my portfolio. Needless to say, I read about all major developments and keep an eye on Directors' share dealings. I also keep an eye on retail sales. Let me give you a recent example — after Psion introduced their new palm-top computer, they had some teething troubles, and a batch had to be withdrawn. While I was interested in the shares, whenever out shopping, I took the opportunity of dropping into a Dixons store and, under the guise of being a prospective customer, asked an assistant how Psion sales were progressing, if they were recommending anything better and whether or not they had had any trouble with the product.

More recently, Psion had some further technical problems, which caused the computer, in a few instances, to lose track of time. One of my broker's clients is a computer buff who acquired a more up-to-date version. He is now well satisfied and has had no further trouble. I also asked a friend who is a computer consultant to buy for me the most up-to-date version of the Series 3, together with the appropriate software, and test it rigorously. He gave me a favourable review.

My anxiety was to establish if the teething troubles were part of normal product enhancement appropriate to break-through technology, or if the product was giving exceptional trouble that was likely to be on-going and costly. I was reassured by the results. If my portfolio had contained one hundred different shares, I would have found it impossible to maintain such a hands-on approach.

You may feel that I have a special advantage in being able to check up on a company in my portfolio. You will in fact be surprised to find that you are probably not more than one or two people away from someone who can give the answers you require. I remember my Chairman at Leyland, Lord Black, saying that when he had his photograph taken for The National Photographic Gallery, he commented to the photographer that he was surprised to find that he knew personally all the famous people in the many photographs hanging on every wall of the studio. The photographer smiled and remarked 'They all say that'. The world is a small place — with just one telephone call, most of those people would have been able to check up on a major new development in many different fields. If you really want to verify something about a company, you will soon find someone who knows someone who can answer your questions. You can also try telephoning the Company Secretary, explain that you are a shareholder, and ask for clarification of any points that may be worrying you. Some Secretaries are very helpful indeed, but they will naturally avoid giving you any 'inside information'.

There is another obvious way of acquiring information about a company in which you have invested — attend the Annual General Meeting. You will find this an interesting experience that will help you to get the feel of the company. Is the meeting well organised? Are the Chairman and the Chief Executive impressive and do they answer questions well? Is the mood of the meeting upbeat or downbeat? These are the kinds of general questions you should ask yourself. If you have any specific ones, that remain unanswered, you can always stand up and fire them at the Chairman.

I mentioned earlier the dreaded words 'inside information'. A grey area that is constantly changing. From the investor's viewpoint, the main thing to avoid is using unpublished and price-sensitive information about a company's future results or a major development such as an impending takeover. Acting upon certain knowledge of a coming unexpected rise or fall in a company's profits is illegal — tips based on this kind of information are therefore obviously best avoided. Takeover tips have an even more inside flavour as the parties involved are under an obligation to make an announcement as soon as they have agreed a deal subject to shareholders' approval (or the predator has unilaterally formed an intention to bid on specific terms).

There is a profound difference between thinking that a company might not be doing so well, after studying the generally available brokers' consensus forecast or national retail sales, and *knowing* from a member of the board that profits are suffering. There is also an obvious difference between concluding that a company might be taken over one day because its assets are grossly under-valued and *knowing* that an acquisitive conglomerate is about to take it over. Acting upon unpublished price-sensitive information is illegal. Acting upon your own judgement based upon generally available facts about a company is fair game and permissible.

There is an old adage on the management of a portfolio — cut losses and run profits. Easy to say but much harder to do. Warren Buffett had a wonderful way of illustrating why you should follow this practice. He took the hypothetical case of being offered the future earnings for life of each and every member of his graduation class. Adapted for the UK, let us take a class of twenty and say that you could have bought all your classmates' life earnings for a fixed sum. Fifteen years elapse before you review the position. Two have died, two are drug addicts, one has A.I.D.S., one is in prison and three are unemployed. Amongst the rest there is a priest, three accountants, two lawyers, a detective sergeant in the police and an actor. The remaining three are really in the money. Of the high-flyers, one is already a captain of industry, another a leading financier and the last one is in line to be Chief Executive of a leading company. If you had to make a few sales at differing prices, would you keep the drop-outs, those who had performed reasonably well or the high-flyers? I know your answer.

Another analogy is of a race-horse owner who has bought ten yearlings for £25,000 each. Seven soon prove hopeless, two quite promising and the last one an absolute star. A successful race-horse of great class can earn good prize money and massive stud fees. Our owner needs to cut down on training costs and stabling expenses and raise a little capital. Which horses should he sell? The hopeless seven followed if necessary by the promising two. He should run his profit on the star.

Pursuing the two analogies of the classmates and the racehorses, it is easy to see when losses should be cut. The reason for selling the drop-outs and the hopeless horses is that *their story has changed*. When you bought the classmates and the yearlings, you may have fancied the prospects of some of them more than others, but you hoped all would succeed. The obvious failures extinguished that hope.

You will remember that in Chapter Six on 'Something New', I made the point that the story of a stock is an important cross-check to which you must continually refer back and check against each new development. Taking a growth stock, for example, if you see that the dividend is only being maintained instead of a more traditional increase you must be alert to a possible slow-down in growth. If several of the executive Directors are selling large parcels of new shares, if the Chairman's statement becomes more cautious, if the relative strength of the stock is very poor, if the Chief Executive you admired suddenly leaves, if the Balance Sheet shows an alarming growth in debt, if you hear of major troubles with the product, if you notice that creative accounting has been at work in a big way — any of these factors might be sufficient to persuade you that the story has changed. *The reasons you bought no longer apply.* The share has become a sell.

The only one of these possible adverse developments that is slightly suspect is the worry about poor relative strength of the share price. Sometimes this happens in isolation for no apparent reason. If the share price falls, arguably, you could buy more stock with exactly the same story that first appealed to you at a substantial discount to your initial purchase price. However, my advice is never to average down.

When shares are performing poorly, I always try to check if there is a big institutional seller. If I can rationalize the fall in price I hold on, but if not I become jittery. As you have probably gathered by now, I am a nervous investor who is very easily frightened. I hate to lose money and on occasions have simply sold because the price action of the shares alarmed me.

There is no formula — you will have to make up your own mind. If you are going to set a cut-off limit for apparently inexplicable losses, I suggest 25% for growth shares, turnarounds and cyclicals and 40% for shells. A formula is not really the answer though. Each share has to be considered on its merits, and both judgement and feel come into play in a big way.

In contrast, if a company's story changes for the worse to a material extent, I *immediately* sell. Speed is of the essence — you want to be first in the queue of disappointed enthusiasts. The share may already have fallen substantially below your purchase price, but that is irrelevant. Cut your loss. You will enjoy a great sense of relief and your portfolio will make for much better viewing.

To my mind, cutting losses is easy and obvious. By far the most difficult task is to decide when to take a profit. At different times in their lives, shares are either a buy, a hold or a sell. You buy a share because it fulfills the criteria of whatever system of investment you are following. As the price increases the share becomes a hold — no longer a buy but not sufficiently matured to become a sell. Turnarounds, cyclicals and asset situations mature more quickly than growth shares. The reason is simple — there is usually a one-off gain to be enjoyed.

As soon as the turnaround has been recognised by one and all, the cyclical has benefited substantially from an up-turn in the economy or shares in the asset situation have appreciated to a level more in line with the underlying worth, the shares should be sold. The status change that you were buying for has been achieved. Now you should look for another share with the same initial potential and try to repeat the process.

Growth shares (and for similar reasons shells) can be very different. If, after a long period of trial and error, you have managed to identify a few excellent growth shares that are churning out earnings per share growth at an exceptional rate of say 20% per annum, you must not let go of them lightly. They might be your ticket to an extraordinary profit. You may have found another Glaxo or Hanson in its infancy.

There are two additional reasons for extending the 'hold' area when the price of a growth share is beginning to mature. The first is the expense of switching. Stamp duty, brokerage and the market makers' turn, both on the share you are selling and the new ones you are buying, might cost you in total as much as 5%-10%, according to the marketability of the shares.

The second factor is capital gains tax. As I have explained, when you take a large profit you crystallize the capital gains tax liability of up to 40% of the gain (less indexation), which is the equivalent of repaying an interest-free loan of that amount to the Government. While you continue to run the profit, the Government is in effect lending you up to

40% of the gain to finance the shares interest-free. Savour this. The more you run the profit the more the Government lends to you.

While on the subject of capital gains tax, I should draw your attention to personal equity plans (PEPs), which were introduced to encourage the general public to invest in quoted companies. They offer a simple way of investing a limited amount of money each year on a tax-free basis — tax can be reclaimed on all dividends and capital gains are free of capital gains tax.

PEPs fall into two categories — general and single company. An individual can invest in each fiscal year up to £6,000 in a general PEP and £3,000 in a single company PEP.

Many investment management companies offer general PEPs through direct mail or advertisements in the national press. The success of these schemes does, of course, depend on the skill of the investment managers, as the investor has no say in the choice of stocks. However, most stockbrokers offer a service to enable investors to run their own schemes and choose their own quoted investments. PEPs are, therefore, an essential tool for anyone using my system of investment, especially for growth shares. A man and his wife can use the full annual limits of £9,000 each. Children cannot be included, unless over eighteen, and all participants must be resident in the UK for tax purposes.

There are very few rules. Your broker will do everything for you — keep the records, look after the share certificates, collect the dividends, advise about rights issues and takeovers and provide you with regular statements. PEP transactions need not be included in your tax returns. There is no limit to the length of time your PEPs need stay in existence. PEPs can be closed at will and all the funds withdrawn, without incurring any tax liability on profits and without the benefit of being able to set off any losses against taxable gains.

Brokers do, of course, charge for their services; typically — £30 for start up, usual dealing commissions, valuation fees of £3 per stock and cancellation fees if you close the account or transfer your PEPs elsewhere.

If you buy a growth share on a PEG factor of 0.75 or less, earnings increase over a year by say 20% and the PEG rises from 0.75 to 1.00, you will enjoy a capital gain of 60%. If the company continues to perform well and looks like a long-term winner, I would, however, hang in there for a little longer and wait until the PEG rises to 1.2. Put in terms of P/E ratios, this would be the equivalent of buying a share growing at 20% per annum on a multiple of 15 and selling when the multiple had risen to 24. After a year, the 20% growth plus the status change in the PEG factor would have almost doubled your money, and you could say to the shares a reluctant *adieu*. Perhaps, on reflection, I should say *au revoir* because having identified a quality share like this, you should keep your eye on the company while you wait for a better moment to repurchase.

You have to bear in mind that with super-growth companies the market often overdoes the hope factor. Really great companies can stand the strain of a very high multiple — they continue to churn out their 20%-25% earnings growth each year so that eventually the fundamentals catch up with the price. Other companies disappoint (perhaps only a little), and their share prices come tumbling down. Erstwhile enthusiasts scramble to find the exit.

You have to try to strike a nice balance between running the profit on a super-growth share and operating within a reasonable safety factor. Perhaps the best way of expressing this is to say that cyclicals, turnarounds and asset situations should be sold on recognition, but with super-growth shares you should wait for adulation.

With shells, as I suggested in Chapter 12, you should run the profit for one year before reviewing the position. There will frequently be very few fundamentals to evaluate. Usually, you have to take a view on the new management team and give them sufficient time to do their job.

The constitution of your portfolio will depend upon the system or systems you have elected to follow. I tend to concentrate upon growth shares and shells. The other major decision you have to make is the amount of cash you intend to hold when you begin to feel bearish. Provided your portfolio is funded with *patient* money, you can afford to remain fully invested. Bull markets climb a wall of worry, and your bearish view might well be wrong. You could easily decide to go liquid and subsequently become fully invested again at just the wrong moment. You may, however, feel more comfortable if you become more liquid at times. In that event, I would recommend a maximum of 50% cash.

Another way of protecting your portfolio is to sell the market as a whole by shorting the FT-SE 100 Index through the futures market or by buying put options. I could write another chapter on this subject alone. The FT-SE 100 Index includes many cyclicals and utilities, so these techniques do not necessarily provide protection for growth stocks, which may perform badly as a sector. On the other hand, the FT-SE 100 Index can usually be sold with the benefit of the contango (imputed interest to the future date of sale). Futures markets can sometimes be very unnerving and frequently move out of kilter with the shares you are trying to hedge. I recommend leaving options and other derivatives to very experienced investors.

Traded options are another growing medium of investment, which by June 1992 applied to 66 top companies. If you are investing in leading stocks, traded options frequently provide a way of obtaining substantial leverage and limiting risk to a few per cent. This is a specialised subject, covered very well in Geoffrey Chamberlain's book — *Trading in Options.*

There is a safety factor in each of the methods of investment I have outlined. This should help to protect you from extreme losses. In a very sharp bear market almost all shares go down, but shares bought in a systematic way will fare better than most. In fact, one of the most reliable tests of an impending bear market is that you will find it extremely difficult to identify shares that fit your highly selective criteria. Many of the shares that were in your portfolio will have been sold because they have fulfilled your objective and are now over the top.

At the risk of over-reminding you about the safety factor, let me reiterate how it applies to all the systems we have examined. Growth shares are being bought on low multiples and low PEG factors — an obvious cushion compared with the market as a whole. In addition, they have to fulfill other rigorous criteria that taken together form a safety net.

Turnarounds and cyclicals should be bought near the bottom, when there is good reason to hope for a recovery or an upturn in the cycle. Another obvious cushion. Turnarounds should be sold when the companies have been turned around and are making good profits. Cyclicals should be sold when there is general recognition that the company has survived the downturn and is enjoying far better trading conditions.

Asset situations should be bought at a substantial discount to realisable values, and should be sold when these values are understood and fully appreciated by other investors. In this case your cushion is the discount on assets and the additional safety net criteria. Of course, the shares can fall in price, but at least you start at a relatively low level with less downside.

Shells are more difficult. Your main safety factor is the selection of a company with top class management, coupled with a small hot air gap and reasonable liquidity. If you are investing mainly in shells and you begin to feel very bearish, I would recommend moving into 50% cash, even if your money is relatively patient. Shells tend to fare very badly in bear markets because a large part of their price is anticipation and hopes for the future. Also, the market in these kinds of shares can suddenly become very narrow and illiquid.

LET ME SUMMARISE FOR YOU THE IMPORTANT POINTS THAT HAVE BEEN MADE IN THIS CHAPTER:

1. Your portfolio should be no more than twelve shares funded by patient money. Ten is the recommended minimum, with a maximum of 15% invested in any one share.

2. Maintain a really hands-on approach after buying. People who can help to answer your questions about your investments know people who know people within your acquaintance. You can also be very active yourself.

3. Run profits and cut losses.

4. Additional factors that make it desirable to run profits are the expenses of switching and the crystallisation of capital gains tax liability if you make a sale. The Government is in effect lending to you the capital gains tax liability interest-free while you run the profit on your shares.

5. Profits should be taken on turnarounds, cyclicals and asset situations when the turnaround is generally acknowledged, the cycle is well advanced, or the share price has appreciated nearer to asset value.

6. Profits on growth shares should be taken more reluctantly. A real gem with earnings continuing to increase at the rate of 20% per annum should be held until the PEG factor is 1.2. You will probably regret selling even then, so keep an eye on the company while you wait for a better moment to repurchase.

7. Profits on shells should be run for a year to give the new management an opportunity to show their paces.

8. Losses should be cut on all shares when the story changes for the worse to such an extent that you would no longer consider buying.

9. If the relative strength of a share is poor, with an apparently inexplicable fall in price, check the market position with your broker. If you cannot find an explanation, you have to use your judgement and feel to decide whether or not to cut the loss. If you are going to adopt a formula for automatically cutting losses, I recommend a 25% limit for turnarounds, cyclicals and growth shares. With shells I suggest losses should be cut if the share price falls by 40%.

10. Your portfolio can be a mixture of the different systems outlined in earlier chapters, but you would probably be better advised to apply The Zulu Principle to one of them.

11. To save capital gains tax, take advantage of self-managed PEPs, especially when investing in dynamic growth companies which you hope to hold as long-term investments.

12. If you feel a bear market is imminent move into up to 50% cash unless your portfolio is easily spared, patient money which you can afford to leave invested through thick and thin. With shell portfolios, you should definitely move into 50% cash if markets are looking dangerous.

13. Leave options, short selling and other derivatives to very experienced investors.

14. There are safety factors in all of the systems I have outlined which should help your portfolio to perform relatively well in both good and bad markets.

18

THE MARKET

EVEN IF IT WAS POSSIBLE TO GIVE YOU A FEW SIMPLE GUIDELINES TO SHOW YOU HOW TO ANTICIPATE A BEAR OR BULL MARKET, THE APPROACH WOULD SOON BE SELF-DEFEATING. As more and more investors followed my successful formula, the market would gradually adjust so that at some future point in time, the formula would become unproductive.

I managed to anticipate the two bear markets of 1973-74 and 1987. In both cases my timing was good but I under-estimated the severity of the eventual decline and closed my short positions far too early. Joseph Granville, the famous American market technician, sums up well the unpredictability of markets. 'Bear markets never visit by appointment ringing your front-door bell by daylight hours. They come like a thief in the night, sneaking in the back-door while the public sleeps the slumber of confidence.'

JOSEPH GRANVILLE

I will attempt to show you how to recognise the top of a bull market and the bottom of a bear market, but whatever your view, you should always have at least 50% of your *patient* money invested in the market. You are at risk of making the wrong judgement about the trend, and you should always remember that selection is far more important than timing. Property experts say that the three important things to remember about investing in property are position, position and position. Investment in shares is very similar, except the key word is selection. This vital point is best illustrated by Coca Cola which became a public company in America in 1919 with a subscription price of $40 per share. The following year sugar prices were up sharply and the price of Coca Cola shares fell below $20. Since then there have been wars, extreme bear markets, recessions, depressions and further major gyrations in the sugar price. Through all these vicissitudes, the original $40 investment has grown to a staggering $1.8m per share. The obvious conclusion is to select the right super-growth stock and stay with it through thick and thin.

Crowd psychology moves markets far more than fundamental values. Greed takes a market up to dizzy heights far beyond real underlying worth. Fear does the opposite.

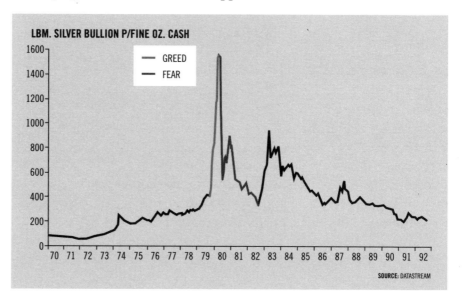

A company's share price moves broadly in sympathy with earnings and/or assets per share, but for several years at a time price and value can be substantially out of kilter. I remember during the seventies Slater Walker had an investment in Poseidon, a company which was purported to have found a major nickel deposit in Australia. I had bought for one of our companies 30,000 shares at just under A$1 each. As they rose daily, I sold 10,000 at A$10, 10,000 at A$20 and the final 10,000 at A$30. I thought I had timed my sales well, only to see the shares rise to over A$100. One Christmas shortly afterwards, I heard from my broker that North Flinders and another small Australian company had found nickel adjacent to the Poseidon deposit. The shares of both companies soared to such a high level that I wondered if there could possibly be enough nickel in the world, never mind Australia, to support the market capitalisations of the three companies. Feeling slightly peeved that I had sold our 30,000 Poseidon shares prematurely, I decided to short North Flinders. A few days later, I had to close our short position after the shares had doubled yet again. Within a few months, Poseidon shares plummeted to about A$4 and North Flinders sank back into obscurity. The point of this story is that I was absolutely right in fundamental terms but my timing was abysmal. If you are intent upon turning a stampede, you have to wait until the cattle are tiring; otherwise you can be trampled underfoot. Manias are very strong indeed and completely ignore fundamental values for long stretches of time. The safest approach is to wait until they have obviously begun to run out of steam.

I have used the word 'mania' deliberately. In a gathering the sentiments and ideas of people begin to take the same direction as their individual conscious personality diminishes. People like to do the 'in' thing and be seen to be doing it — to eat at the 'in' restaurant, to see the 'in' play and to be able to say they have read the 'in' book. According to Le Bon in his famous book *The Crowd*, 'A collective mind is formed, doubtless transitory, but presenting very clearly defined characteristics. The gathering has become ... a psychological crowd. Crowds being only capable of thinking in images are only impressed by images.' An image such as the possibility of acquiring *instant wealth* is easy to understand and far more appealing than a few boring and perhaps rather depressing fundamentals. An image as strong as instant wealth would be sufficient to carry a crowd beyond sanity into mania.

Charles Mackay, in his excellent book *Extraordinary Popular Delusions and the Madness of Crowds*, gives examples of the Mississippi Scheme and the South Sea Bubble. Tulipomania has always been my favourite. In the early seventeenth century, many people in Holland were collecting tulips to such an extent that it was proof of bad taste for a man of fortune to be without a rare tulip bulb collection. The desire to possess tulip bulbs spread to the Dutch middle classes. By the year 1636, the demand for rare tulip bulbs increased so much that regular marts for their sale were established on the Stock Exchange in many of the principal cities. As prices continued to rise, many individuals who had speculated in tulips suddenly became very rich. People in all walks of life began to convert their hard-earned money into tulip bulbs. Tulipomania became rampant.

You may wonder how the Dutch people allowed themselves to be so carried away from reality. Your wonderment would have been shared by an unfortunate sailor who stole a tulip bulb from a merchant's store, thinking that it was an onion, which a few hours later he ate with his herring breakfast. The tulip bulb in question was a Semper Augustus then worth about 3000 Florins, which would have been sufficient to feed his entire ship's crew for over a year. The poor fellow had plenty of time to think about tulip bulbs during the months he spent in prison on the felony charge.

After a while, some of the more conservative rich people began to have some doubts. They ceased buying bulbs and began to sell a few. The worry spread, confidence was lost, and prices tumbled, never to recover. At the height of the mania a Semper Augustus tulip bulb commanded a price of 5500 Florins. The low price, after a 99% fall, was a mere 50 Florins. With many extreme manias, investors lose about 90% of their investment after the bubble has burst.

The cycle of a financial mania is easy to understand:

1. An image of instant wealth attracts and forms the financial, psychological 'crowd'.

2. People see what they want to see — a mixture of both facts and fancy which builds an image in their minds. A few examples of exceptional gains in the new area of interest are put forward as being representative of the kind of profits that can be made by one and all.

3. Acknowledged experts in the field urge the crowd on its way.

4. The crowd begins to act irrationally and becomes blind to danger, ignoring fundamentals and all traditional measures of value. Throughout these developments, prices continue to rise rapidly — a self-feeding process that encourages more and more buyers to participate.

5. As if a new slide has been placed in the projector, the image that has attracted and formed the financial crowd is suddenly changed.

6. Fear replaces greed as the bubble bursts with disastrous financial consequences for those who invested anywhere near the top.

The most amazing feature of the whole process is that people never seem to learn from the mistakes that were made during previous manias. The main reason is, of course, the difficulty of being able to resist being drawn into the psychological crowd.

It is very important for you to realise that financial manias are not just an academic subject about events like Tulipomania that happened many years ago to other people who were silly. People are still silly today. In 1987, at the top of the utility boom, the Japanese Government floated NTT, the Japanese telephone monopoly. The price was Y1.6m per share on a multiple of 170 times earnings, with a dividend yield of 0.3%. At the peak price of Y3.18m the shares were quoted at about 340 times earnings, and the valuation of NTT was more than the entire German stockmarket.

Since then the Japanese bubble has well and truly burst. NTT was a leading example of a mania in full cry. By June 1992, the price had fallen to Y581,000 on a prospective multiple of 67 times 1993 earnings. With a further decline in earnings forecast for 1994, the shares still look very expensive.

Another recent but far less extreme example occurred with property in London in the late eighties. My younger son impressed me when he was working in the dealing room of a commodity brokers in 1988, during a spell between school and university. He came home one evening and announced confidently that we were almost at the end of the residential property boom in the UK. 'They are all talking about getting their feet on the property ladder and how much they have made so far,' he said. 'They cannot even imagine property going the other way.' He was right. I wish I had listened to him more attentively.

There are a number of ways of testing if a market is in a bullish or bearish phase. For example, when the bull is rampant, shares usually sell on historically high P/E ratios and at large premiums to book value. Furthermore, there is a high degree of speculation and a plethora of new issues of dubious value. But you have to understand that the bear is a wily animal, and each market cycle has subtle variations from previous ones. It would all be too simple if the bear was easy to recognise — he is out to trap you, so you can be sure that most people will not see him coming. Keep this warning firmly in your mind, while I set out for you some of the more traditional signals that have heralded the top of *previous* bull markets and the bottom of *previous* bear markets. As you will quickly see, bull and bear market signals are like the reverse sides of the same coin.

SIGNS OF THE TOP OF A BULL MARKET

CASH IS TRASH

In early April 1992, this was the consensus view of a large number of American fund managers, who coined the phrase. The consequent very low institutional cash holdings are an obvious danger signal for that market.

VALUE IS HARD TO FIND

The average P/E ratio of the market as a whole will be near to historically high levels. The average dividend yield will be low and shares will be standing at a high premium to book values. If you have been following my systems,you will have already sold many shares and very few will measure up to your criteria.

Our June 1992 Datastream analysis of leading shares proved to me that bargains were hard to find in the FT-SE 100 Index. The American market is unquestionably at a very high level in relation to historic precedents of value.

SIGNS OF THE BOTTOM OF A BEAR MARKET

CASH IS KING

At the bottom of a bear market, it is universally recognised that cash is the best possible asset to own. Institutional cash holdings are therefore usually at very high levels.

VALUE IS EASY TO FIND

The average P/E ratio of the market as a whole will be near to historically low levels. The average dividend yield will be high and shares may be standing at a discount to book values.

In January 1975, at the bottom of the bear market the FT Ordinary Share Index stood at 146, the lowest it had been since May 1954. The average P/E ratio was under 4 with a dividend yield of over 13%; ICI yielded 13.4%, Glynwed 24%, Tarmac 17.7% and Lex Service 43.6%.

TECHNICAL ANALYSIS SIGNALS

Brian Marber tells me that head and shoulders patterns, double tops, triangles and wedges are *sometimes* found at the top of bull markets. The signal he prefers to work on is Momentum Thrust. For example, when over 75% of all stocks in a market have been standing above their long-term average, if they turn below 75% that is a significant signal. In late June 1992, this has just happened in London.

Another important and more anticipatory indicator is Coppock, which usually gives excellent buy signals. Presently Coppock is giving no such signal.

INTEREST RATES

Interest rates are usually about to rise or have already started to do so. UK rates were last reduced in May 1992, but Germany's problems limit the scope for further action. In the USA, rates continue to be cut by the Federal Reserve, but this cannot go on for ever. After the Presidential Election, rates will probably rise again.

MONEY SUPPLY

Broad money supply tends to be contracting at the turn of bull markets.

INVESTMENT ADVISORS

The consensus view of investment advisors will be bullish.

NEW ISSUES

Offers for sale, rights issues and new issues are usually in abundance, with quality suffering and low grade issues being chased to ridiculous levels. In June 1992, the UK new issue market looked as if it might become more active, but in the USA conditions had been very frothy and were just beginning to calm down as investors became more circumspect.

TECHNICAL ANALYSIS SIGNALS

Brian Marber tells me that head and shoulders reverse patterns, double bottoms, triangles and wedges are *sometimes* found at the bottom of bear markets. The Momentum Thrust indicator works to identify a coming upswing in the market when under 25% of stocks are above their moving averages and the percentage turns upwards.

At the bottom of a bear market, you look for an upturn in the Coppock indicator, which is usually a strong buy signal.

INTEREST RATES

Interest rates are *usually* at a high level and are about to fall or have just begun to do so. At the bottom of the 1981/2 bear market, for example, the long bond in America was yielding a staggeringly high 15.23%.

MONEY SUPPLY

Broad money supply tends to be increasing at the turn of bear markets.

INVESTMENT ADVISORS

The consensus view of investment advisors will be bearish.

NEW ISSUES

There will be hardly a new issue in sight. Entrepreneurs, who have built up private companies to a size sufficient to obtain a public quotation, wait for better markets to obtain better prices for their businesses.

INSIDER TRADING

The ratio of insider selling to buying is often at a high level. However, it is important to note that insiders are not always right — they are also part of the psychological crowd.

REACTION TO NEWS

An early sign of a bull market topping out is the failure of shares to respond to good news. The Directors of a company might report excellent results only to see the price of their shares fall. The market is becoming exhausted, good news is already discounted and there is very little buying power left.

CHANGES IN MARKET LEADERSHIP

Drug companies have been a favourite for many years, and companies like Glaxo have become established as market leaders. In the sixties, conglomerates were the flavour of the decade, in the early seventies, financial and property companies, and in the late seventies, oil companies. A major change in leadership is often a prelude to a change in market direction.

At the top of the bull market investors usually move from safe growth stocks into cyclicals which they buy heavily.

PARTY TALK

At the peak of a bull market, shares tend to be a main topic of conversation at cocktail and dinner parties. In America, New York taxi drivers frequently volunteer details of their portfolios and give unsolicited views on the market.

INSIDER TRADING

The ratio of insider buying to selling will be at a higher level. However it is important to note that insiders are not always right — they are also part of the psychological crowd.

REACTION TO NEWS

An early sign of a bear market bottoming is the failure of shares to fall on bad news. The market will have already discounted the results, and there will be very little further selling to come.

CHANGES IN MARKET LEADERSHIP

Sectors that have had many years of unpopularity have been busy building a solid technical base, and may begin to show signs of life, which could indicate that they might be the leaders in the next bull market. For example, gold and other resource stocks have been out of fashion for many years now. *All the world's* quoted gold mines do not add up to the market capitalisation of Glaxo, so very little buying would be needed to spark off a boom in gold shares again.

At the bottom of a bear market, growth stocks become dirt cheap as multiples crumble.

PARTY TALK

The prevailing mood will be so dismal that most people will believe that there is no longer much point in owning shares. In a bear market, no-one wants to talk about the Stock Exchange.

MEDIA COMMENT

The press and TV tend to give more prominence to the stock market and to be optimistic near the top. If prices appear high in relation to value, the argument is that 'it will be different this time'. The few bearish articles that warn of dangers to come are ignored by investors.

OTHER USA MEASURES

There are a number of other indicators that are more readily obtainable in the USA than in the UK. The most popular ones are the following:

a) Calls to puts ratio
The higher the ratio of calls, the more speculative the financial climate.

b) The odd lot indicators
Odd lotters are investors who buy or sell in less than round lots of one hundred shares. The theory is that they are less well informed. If they are buying heavily they will probably be wrong and the market will be due for a correction.

c) Short interest ratio
A low ratio of short selling to total volume on the NYSE is often a sign that a bull market is due for a fall. Short sellers are professionals who should know what they are doing, but they are also part of the psychological crowd.

d) Mutual funds
Early in 1992, $7bn a month was pouring into aggressive mutual funds from American investors who were transferring their savings from money market funds because of falling interest rates. The mutual funds found it easy to attract these savings by drawing attention to the spectacular returns on money invested in the American stock market over the *past* ten years. Most mutual funds invest from 80% to 100% of their available cash, so this enormous influx of money had to be placed in the market, driving prices to dizzy heights. If the public is disillusioned and redemptions begin in a big way, it will be curtains for the bull market.

MEDIA COMMENT

Press and TV comment shrinks in response to lack of public interest. The odd bullish article is ignored (probably on the grounds that the journalist who wrote it is demented).

OTHER USA MEASURES

The opposite side of the coin for the other indicators, which are readily obtainable in the USA, is as follows:

a) Calls to puts ratio
The higher the ratio of puts, the more bearish the financial climate. In this kind of atmosphere a rebound is very likely.

b) The odd lot indicators
If odd lotters are selling heavily that can be a bullish signal heralding a possible end to the bear market.

c) Short interest ratio
A bear market can turn very sharply indeed when there is a massive short interest position in the market. At the slightest hint of good news, short sellers would be quick to cover. As they repurchased, prices would rise dramatically, creating a buying panic amongst them.

d) Mutual funds
When mutual fund redemptions slow down to a more normal level and the flow of money from investors begins to turn quietly positive, a firm base will be provided to fuel a major uplift in share prices. In this kind of financial climate, most mutual funds will tend to have larger cash balances to meet future redemptions and because the managers feel bearish. The market will be over-sold, so very little buying would have a dramatic impact on share prices.

There are a few general points to be made about bull and bear markets:

a)   You will be pleased to know that bull markets usually last longer than bear markets.

b)   Bull markets take many years to build and then a long time to move from the massive over-valuations caused by greed to the substantial under-valuations that usually prevail in the fearsome conditions of a major bear market.

c)   A great deal of money can be lost in a very short time in a vicious bear market. The average fall in the seven bear markets since 1964 was 34%, lasting an average of 57 weeks, but in 1973-75 the fall was 73% for a very unhappy 136 weeks.

d)   Bull markets frequently seem to last four to five years, which may have some connection with electoral cycles. There are many exceptions however.

e)   To my mind, there is no real difference between a major correction in a bull market and a mini-bear market. I suppose a technical purist would argue that after the 1987 crash the market recovered and went above its previous high, suggesting that the bull market was still intact, and 1987 was simply a major correction.

   A major bear market is different — a prolonged period of at least nine months and sometimes as much as two to three years, during which bearish conditions prevail and you wish you were somewhere else.

f)   In the eighties, global markets seemed to move in step. During the days after the 1987 crash, one afternoon Wall Street might fall sharply, with a knock-on effect in Tokyo overnight — which in turn would weaken opening prices in London the next morning. But less than five years later, Japan had more than halved, while both Wall Street and London had reached all-time highs.

   In the final analysis, no major country can succeed in isolation. If the world economy falls into a deep recession, there is no doubt that every major stockmarket will be affected. Nevertheless, there does seem to be more scope today for a number of individual stock-markets to rise, even if some of the other major markets in the world are in a down-trend.

g) Both bull and bear markets have several different stages. In a bear market for example, stage 1 is usually a sharp fall during which economic conditions remain positive.

In stage 2 economic conditions deteriorate but the market becomes over-sold. There is then a sucker rally, powerful enough to persuade most investors into believing that the market has bottomed. During stage 3, the economic news becomes awful. Investors panic and sell at any price. The market declines very sharply as the downward spiral becomes self-feeding. Stage 3 is only over and ready as a springboard for the next bull market when investors abandon all hope for the future. The first positive sign will be that shares no longer fall on bad news.

All this makes for very gloomy reading, but it is important for you to realise that markets can go down as well as up. Remember that vicious bear markets carry almost everything down with them irrespective of underlying value, so do not try to beat the trend. Wait until the storm passes.

HERE IS A SUMMARY OF MY ADVICE ON GENERAL MARKET STRATEGY:

1. By reading your daily and weekly newspapers, investment magazines and newsletters you should be able to keep your finger on the pulse of the market.

2. You have seen the table of warning signals and must make up your own mind on the state of the general market.

3. If you feel bullish, invest 100% of your *patient* money. If bearish, 50%.

4. When pruning your portfolio down from 100% to 50% keep your more defensive stocks. This should happen naturally as you sell shares which fulfill your investment objectives. With a growth portfolio, keep the shares on the lower PEG factors. You do not mind the multiple remaining high, provided the growth is still there to support the price.

5. Do not consider shorting stocks unless you are a full time professional. You can so easily be right about the fundamentals but horribly wrong with the timing — remember North Flinders.

6. Avoid options and other derivatives unless you are an experienced investor. These financial instruments have all the attractions and drawbacks of investments that are very highly geared. You can make a great deal of money or lose all you have invested.

7. Above all, do not allow a bear market to frighten you into taking your patient money out of your carefully selected super-growth shares that are continuing to perform well. Remember the Coca Cola story — $40 to $1.8m per share; £1000 to £45m in an average man's lifetime. That is what investment is all about.

19

TEN GUIDELINES

YOU MAY HAVE HEARD OF IAN LITTLE, AN OXFORD UNIVERSITY PROFESSOR, WHO WROTE A PAPER IN 1962 ON THE UNPREDICTABILITY OF EARNINGS ENTITLED *'HIGGLEDY PIGGLEDY GROWTH'*. He argued that forecasting earnings was unreliable and that the earnings trends of a large number of British companies had been of no use in predicting their future course.

Little was criticised, his work was revised but still appeared to prove that earnings followed a random walk of their own, showing no correlation between past and future rates of growth. Put another way, Little was saying that in a fast-moving world, constantly changing industrial, economic, political and competitive conditions make it virtually impossible to use the past as a reliable guide to the future.

I like Ian Little, whom I have met on several occasions. His paper was well researched, but I do not agree with his conclusion, which is at odds with the records of companies like Coca Cola, Glaxo, Wellcome and Rentokil.

Ian Little's basic argument can also be turned around to make an important point to you. If it is accepted that predicting future earnings is difficult, if not impossible, you must surely agree that there must be an advantage in buying shares *in a systematic way* — shares with excellent growth records that satisfy highly selective criteria and have a built-in safety factor. Why gamble on shares with relatively high P/E ratios if you cannot rely upon earnings forecasts and trends? If you have no idea what is going to happen to future earnings, you might as well play safe and buy a share that appears to be very cheap in relation to present earnings and the known facts. At least try to get value for your money.

The analysis of the FT-SE 100 Index in Chapter Fourteen showed that the best performing companies all shared the competitive advantage of a strong business franchise, evidenced by their excellent rate of return on capital employed. It is no coincidence that companies like these perform well — it is glaringly obvious that they are likely to do so. There is nothing higgledy piggledy about their growth.

It also pays to be systematic with your investment policy so that you have a base to refer back to when measuring your performance. If your results prove unsatisfactory, your system can then be modified. By concentrating and focusing your investment approach, you should become more and more expert in the particular method you have chosen.

Without doubt a systematic approach works. Needless to say, a few minor details, like having the right system and the right person operating it, are essential pre-requisites, but, given these, the results can be spectacular. I can support this argument with my own experience as an investor, the performance of the Capitalist portfolio, an American study by Professor Marc Reinganum and the well documented performance over many years of the major followers of Ben Graham. Common sense also tells me that, pitted against a random walker or a darts player, I would stand a far better chance by buying carefully selected shares that have the extra ingredient of a substantial safety factor such as a relatively low P/E ratio in relation to their proven growth rate, or in the case of a shell, excellent management and strong liquidity. I also believe that with growth shares and shells, the logic of systematically running profits and cutting losses is indisputable, and that a hands-on approach to investment will always beat a more casual one.

A hundred or more points have been made in earlier chapters, so any summary must inevitably leave out the majority of them. At the risk of over-simplification, I will end on the note of suggesting ten very broad and basic guidelines which should help you to improve your investment performance:

1. Select a system of investment that suits your temperament and concentrate upon it. Whichever system you choose, the essential ingredient must be that the shares you select provide you with a margin of safety — a safety factor created by the very stringent criteria of your system.

2. Set aside at least three hours a week to apply The Zulu Principle to your chosen system so that you become an expert in that relatively narrow area of the market. Use most of the time for analysis and always read the accounts of selected companies from beginning to end. Refine and improve your system as you learn from both your successes and your mistakes.

3. Allocate from your available resources a sum to invest — patient money that you can spare and afford. Your aim is to avoid being pressurised into having to make a premature sale.

    Invest between 50% and 100% of your patient money at all times. When you believe the outlook to be exceptionally bearish you can reduce your investments to 50% of your portfolio if you feel more comfortable doing so. With a shell company system in a very bearish climate you should definitely move into 50% cash.

4. Choose a broker who understands your objectives and is out to help you. Your broker can be an invaluable ally.

5. Invest in a maximum of twelve shares which meet your criteria. Ten is the recommended mimimum, with a maximum investment of 15% in any one share.

6. With any system based on small to medium-sized growth stocks, you are seeking to identify a few super-growth shares and hold on to them through thick and thin. Selection is far more important than timing. Buy shares which have low P/E ratios in relation to their growth rates and consequently low PEG factors — not more than 0.75 and preferably below 0.66.

    You are searching for companies with strong business franchises that enjoy an excellent return on capital employed and generate plenty of cash. In addition, you must ensure that the other criteria set out in detail in earlier chapters are satisfied to a sufficient extent to provide you with an adequate safety net.

    Always reconcile a selected company's trading profits with its net operating cash flow. Remember that cash is the only indisputable asset and that when making an investment you should look down first.

7. After you have purchased a share, maintain a really hands-on

approach. You will soon find someone who knows someone who can answer your questions about most companies. Be very active in monitoring your portfolio.

8. Growth shares should be sold if the market goes mad and in the process awards any of your investments an absurd multiple. With smaller companies, you should plan to exit when the PEG is around 1.2, but subsequently keep an eye on excellent growth stocks in the hope of finding a better opportunity to repurchase them.

9. The converse of running profits is to cut losses. Shares should be sold the moment the story changes to such an extent that the shares no longer satisfy your buying criteria. There are also other signals for selling, such as major sales of stock by Directors. Be disciplined about this.

10. With turnarounds, cyclicals and asset situations you have more limited investment objectives. Once the crowd recognises that a company has been turned around, that the cycle is well on the way up again or that a share price better reflects the underlying asset value, you will usually find that the share has appreciated sufficiently to provide you with a graceful and profitable exit.

    With shells a different approach is needed. They are similar in many ways to growth shares, but some will never make the grade. Excellent management, strong City support and reasonable liquidity are the key criteria.

In the foregoing chapters you have been given a back-cloth of investment know-how on such important subjects as PEGs, competitive advantage, creative accounting, liquidity and relative strength. The better you understand the essentials of investment, the better your judgement is likely to be and the more likely you will be to develop a feel for the market and an instinct for financial self-preservation. You must apply The Zulu Principle. The more you read about investment, the more you think about it, the more you talk to people who really know the subject and the more work you put into monitoring your shares, the 'luckier' you will become and the better your investments will perform.

20

GLOSSARY

MOST GLOSSARIES ARE A LIST OF DEFINITIONS, AND FOR THAT REASON
ARE NOT EASY TO READ. I prefer to begin with the description of a hypothetical company, in which you will come across most of the terms and
expressions you would find in a normal glossary. Afterwards, in case
you should have any residual doubts, I have repeated the more important definitions and added a few more that might be of interest to you.

We will name the company Feelgood plc. We will assume that it is
in the health food business and has 10 million shares in issue. The
shares are quoted publicly and valued in the stockmarket at £1 each.
The *market capitalisation* of Feelgood is therefore £10 million (10
million shares multiplied by £1).

The underlying *net assets* (shops, fixtures and fittings, stock and
debtors less the amount owing to creditors) of Feelgood are worth say
£7m, giving a *net asset value per share* of 70p (£7m divided by 10
million shares). The profits of Feelgood for the current financial year are
£1m before tax. The effective tax rate was 33%, giving *profits after tax*
of £670,000 (£1m of pre tax profits less 33% corporation tax).

The net profits of Feelgood of £670,000 are also called the net
earnings of the company. The *earnings per share (EPS)* of Feelgood are
6.7p (£670,000 divided by the 10 million shares in issue). As Feelgood's
shares stand at £1 in the market, they are priced at 16 times earnings
(16 times 6.7p equals 100p). The ratio of the price of the shares of 100p
to the earnings per share of 6.7p is called the *price earnings ratio*.
Feelgood therefore has a price earnings ratio of 16. An abbreviation for
price earnings ratio is *P/E ratio* or as it is sometimes called, *the multiple*.

If Feelgood decided to pay a dividend of 2.1p per share, the *dividend
yield* of Feelgood shares would be calculated by first adding back the

basic rate of income tax (say 25%), which it is assumed has been paid, and expressing the answer as a percentage of the share price. The calculation is made in two stages as follows:

$$\frac{2.1\text{p} \times 100}{75} = 2.8\text{p} \text{ which is the } gross \ dividend.$$

The dividend yield is therefore

$$\frac{2.8 \text{ (the gross dividend)}}{100 \text{ (the share price)}} \times 100 = 2.8\%.$$

If the shares rose from £1 to £2 the dividend yield would fall to

$$\frac{(2.8 \times 100)}{200} = 1.4\%$$

With earnings per share of 6.7p, Feelgood could have paid a higher dividend. The board, however, decided to be prudent, and as a result the *dividend cover* was 3.2 times (6.7p earnings per share divided by the dividend of 2.1p).

Feelgood would be shown in the prices section of the *Financial Times* like this:

	Price	High	Low	Market Cap £m	Yield Gross	P/E
		1992				
FEELGOOD	100	140	75	10	2.8	16

If the Directors of Feelgood need to raise further funds, they might arrange for a *rights issue*, offering all existing shareholders the right to buy one more share at a price of say 80p for every four shares owned at present. This particular rights issue would raise £2m (10 million divided by four, multiplied by 80p).

If the Directors were doubtful about all the shareholders taking up their rights, they might decide to *underwrite* the issue through their stockbrokers or *merchant bankers* (specialist banks which advise on takeovers, flotations and other financial deals), who would arrange for a number of *institutions* (insurance companies, pension funds etc) and perhaps some private clients to agree to buy any of the shares not subscribed for by existing Feelgood shareholders. In exchange, the broker or merchant banker would be paid an *underwriting fee*, a substantial proportion of which would be passed on to the institutions and private clients who agreed to take up the shares.

At a later stage of Feelgood's development, the shares might rise to as much as £10 each. The Directors might then decide that the shares were too 'heavy' and that there would be a more liquid market in them if they were priced substantially lower and there was a larger number in issue. To achieve this happier state of affairs they might arrange for a one for one *scrip issue*, which means that existing shareholders would be given one free share for each share they own. The shareholders would then own two shares instead of one, and, as a result, there would be double the number of shares in issue. Strictly on the arithmetic, the share price should fall to £5 after the issue, so in a sense the shareholder would not be any better off. However, scrip issues are often accompanied by dividend increases, and are usually made by expanding companies. After they are split, shares appear to be cheaper, so they frequently perform better than the market as a whole.

In an expanding phase, the Directors may not want to *dilute* Feelgood's share capital (by issuing more shares), so if they need further funds they might decide to borrow from the company's bankers or raise a *debenture*. A debenture is a loan which is usually secured on particular assets of a company like factories and machinery, and carries a fixed rate of interest. The interest payable on the debenture would be paid out of the profits, or, if the company was losing money, be added to losses. If the debenture interest fell into arrears, the debenture holders would have the right to appoint a *Receiver*, who would move into the company and take charge of the secured assets with a view to selling them off to repay the debenture holders. In that event, or if the company went into liquidation, the debenture would be repaid first (well before other creditors) out of the proceeds of the sale of the secured assets.

A softer alternative to a debenture would be a *convertible loan stock*, which would not be secured on any particular assets, and in the event of a *liquidation* (when a liquidator, usually an accountant, is appointed to wind up a company) would rank after debenture holders but before ordinary shareholders. The interest payable, which is usually less than debenture interest, would also be paid as a charge against profits before any dividends were paid to shareholders. In exchange for having less security and lower interest than a debenture, the convertible loan stockholders would have the right at specified future dates to convert their convertible loan stocks into ordinary shares. Convertibles are often issued on takeovers to avoid too much argument about the worth of the shares being offered, and to offer a more advantageous yield to shareholders in the target company.

Another, even softer, alternative to raising further funds would be a *convertible preference share*. At one time, this was classified as part of the capital of a business, but nowadays if there is a *redemption date* (a set date for repayment) the preference shares would rank as debt. In the event of a liquidation, the capital of convertible preference shareholders would be repaid before ordinary shareholders, but after all the debentures, convertibles, loan stocks and other creditors. The dividend payable to convertible preference shareholders would only be paid after all other interest payments.

If Feelgood was a larger company, it would have a further option for raising funds — the issue of an *unsecured loan stock*. In a liquidation these rank behind debentures but before convertible loan stocks and before other creditors. An unsecured loan stockholder has no right to convert into ordinary shares, and, as the stock is also less secure than a debenture, would usually enjoy a higher rate of interest. Only very strong companies can issue unsecured loan stocks, which are unappealing to the general run of investors.

Preference shares without any conversion rights would also be unpopular with institutions because Feelgood is a small company and the institutions are not particularly keen on preference shares as they do not confer the right to participate in future profits. For capital repayment, preference shares rank before ordinary shareholders in a liquidation, and their fixed dividend is payable before a dividend can be paid on the ordinary shares. Sometimes a preference share is designated a *cumulative preference share*, which means that the dividend is accrued, if passed in any year. When a company is brought back from the dead by radical reorganisation or a stroke of good fortune, a cumulative preference share can sometimes be very valuable because of the accumulated dividend arrears, which have to be paid as the company begins to make profits again.

A small company like Feelgood would almost certainly be quoted on the *Unlisted Securities Market (USM)*, which is, in effect, the second tier of the market. Companies trading on this are usually much smaller and have had to measure up to less onerous listing requirements than those with a full listing. In particular, they only need a two year record of trading profits.

Companies like Rentokil, Glaxo, Sainsbury and Next are *listed*, which means that they have satisfied the Stock Exchange's criteria for a quotation on the full market. Any transaction in these shares would appear in the *Official List*.

If you wanted to buy some shares in Feelgood, your first step would be to open an account with a *broker* (who would act as your agent in buying and selling stocks). Once your broker knew you, he or she would take your order by telephone. If you decided to buy 1000 shares in Feelgood for say 100p each, you would ask your broker the price for 1000 shares, which might be 98p-102p. This means that the *market maker* (a firm offering to act as a principal and buy or sell shares for their own account) would be prepared to sell 1000 shares in Feelgood at 102p *(the offer price)* and buy at 98p *(the bid price)*. In fact, your broker would also check with other market makers to give you the keenest overall price for buying or selling. The difference between the bid price and the offer price is called the *bid-offer spread*, which in this case would be 4p.

As soon as the *bargain* (transaction) was completed your broker would send you a *Contract Note* which, in addition to the price of the shares purchased, would include Stamp Duty of 0.5% and the broker's commission, which would be negotiable, ranging from 1.65% to under 0.5%, according to the amount of business you transact. You would then receive the broker's statement and in due course you would receive a *Share Certificate* for your 1000 shares in Feelgood.

The buying and selling of shares takes place within the *Account*, which normally lasts two weeks but occasionally three. The Account period runs from Monday to the Friday, either eleven or eighteen days later. All deals done in the Account are settled on the second Monday after the final Friday.

A few months after the end of Feelgood's financial year, the company would make a preliminary announcement (key information on the full year's results, which is notified to the Stock Exchange and usually carried by the press the following day) of profits, taxation and dividends for the previous year. A few weeks later, you would receive the Annual Report and Accounts which embellishes the stark details and usually contains a forecast or an indication of trading expectations for the year ahead.

Let us examine the Report and Accounts of Feelgood. The May 1992 *Consolidated Balance Sheet* (consolidated accounts include the results of all companies in the group to give the complete picture) looked like this:

CONSOLIDATED BALANCE SHEET

	1992 £000
FIXED ASSETS	
Intangible assets	500
Tangible assets	5000
Investments	–
	5500
CURRENT ASSETS	
Stocks	8500
Debtors	1000
Cash in hand	2000
	11500
CREDITORS	
Amounts falling due within one year	7000
NET CURRENT ASSETS	4500
TOTAL ASSETS LESS CURRENT LIABILITIES	10000
CREDITORS	
Amounts falling due after more than one year	2750
PROVISIONS	
Deferred taxation	250
MINORITY INTERESTS	–
	3000
NET ASSETS EMPLOYED	7000

	£000
CAPITAL AND RESERVES	
Called-up share capital	2500
Profit and loss account	4500
SHAREHOLDERS' FUNDS	7000

Under the Companies Act 1985, the *Fixed Assets* have to be shown in three categories:

1. INTANGIBLE ASSETS, which are usually brand names, copyrights, trademarks and goodwill. The kinds of assets that are rather nebulous, although in many cases very valuable.

2. TANGIBLE ASSETS, which are those held by a business for the purpose of earning its profits — they are therefore usually not for sale. These fixed assets include land and buildings, plant and machinery and motor vehicles. In the case of Feelgood, they would include shop freeholds and leases and fixtures and fittings. Precise details are given in the detailed Notes to the Accounts, which also show the amount of *depreciation* (the amount set aside to cover the eventual replacement of an asset) which has been written off to arrive at the book value.

3. INVESTMENTS, which are essentially long-term investments not being held with a view to resale.

We then come to the *Current Assets*, which include cash and any other assets, like stocks and debtors, that will eventually be turned into cash in the normal course of business. In the case of a manufacturing company, the first item, *Stocks*, would be broken down into three categories in the notes: raw materials, work in progress and finished goods. *Debtors* would also be analysed in some detail between trade and other debtors and prepayments. *Cash* is one of those delightful assets that needs no further description.

Creditors have to be shown under two headings — the amounts falling due within one year and the amounts falling due after one year. The detailed Notes to the Accounts usually show the first category in great detail. With Feelgood, they would include bank overdraft (if any), trade creditors, current corporation tax, accruals and deferred income, other loans and the dividend payable.

The difference between Current Assets and Current Liabilities is the *Net Current Assets*. There is then the further total of Total Assets less Current Liabilities, which in this case is £10m. The only amounts that need to be deducted from this total to arrive at the *Net Assets Employed* in the business are the following:

1. CREDITORS - amounts falling due after more than one year. The Notes to the Accounts set these out in detail. With Feelgood, the total of £2.75m would include long-term bank loans (if any), mortgages, obligations under finance leases and hire purchase contracts and other long-term loans.

2. PROVISIONS - any amounts retained to cover any liability or loss which is likely to be incurred. In this case there was only deferred taxation of £250,000.

3. MINORITY INTERESTS - represent the share of the assets of the business in subsidiaries that are not wholly owned. There are none in Feelgood.

The Net Assets Employed therefore amount to £7m in total (£10m less £3m). The shareholders own these assets through their shareholdings. There are 10 million ordinary shares in issue with a par value of 25p resulting in *Called-up Share Capital* of £2.5m. In this instance, as in many others, shareholders' original capital investment has been supplemented by profits (£4.5m) ploughed back over the years.

The Consolidated Profit and Loss Account for the year ended 31st May 1992 is also very straightforward. Against each major figure there is usually a number relating to a more detailed explanation in the Notes to the Accounts. The Turnover, for example, is analysed in some detail, and there is another note showing that the Trading Profit is stated after charging Directors' emoluments of £160,000, auditors' remuneration of £40,000 and other items of particular interest.

There is also a Cash Flow Statement. In Chapter Five, I explain how important it is to ensure that the company's Operating (or Trading) Profits are broadly in line with net cash inflow from operating (or trading) activities. You will quickly learn how to focus upon the important figures in the Report and Accounts and pay less attention to some of the less relevant ones.

If, after reading the definitions that follow, you have any residual doubts, I suggest that before starting my book you read a primer on investment. I recommend Bernard Gray's *Beginners' Guide to Investment* — you should pay particular attention to Chapter Fifteen on valuing shares.

CONSOLIDATED PROFIT AND LOSS ACCOUNT

	1992 £000
Turnover	6000
Cost of sales	3000
Gross profit	3000
Selling and distribution costs	1200
Administrative expenses	750
	1950
Trading profit	1050
Interest receivable	–
	1050
Interest payable	50
	1000
Taxation	330
Profit for the financial year	670
Minority interests	–
Profits attributable to shareholders	670
Dividends paid and proposed	210
Amounts transferred to reserves	460
Earnings per ordinary share	6.7p

DEFINITIONS RELATED TO THE VALUATION OF QUOTED SHARES

1. DIVIDEND YIELD - The dividend yield of a company can be determined by dividing the gross annual dividend into the share price. If a company paid 10p a share gross dividend and the shares were 100p, the dividend yield would be 10%. If the price rose to 200p, the dividend yield would be reduced to 5%.

    Dividend yields can be both historic and prospective. The historic dividend yield is based upon last year's dividend payment, whereas the prospective dividend yield is based upon the dividend forecast by the Directors for the year ahead. Dividends are usually paid twice yearly, with an interim payment after the end of the half year and the final payment after the full year's accounts are available. The dividend yield of a company is based upon the total dividends paid or payable by the company in a given year.

2. MARKET CAPITALISATION - The total number of shares the company has in issue multiplied by the share price, which is constantly changing.

3. THE PRICE EARNINGS RATIO - The number of times earnings per share need to be multiplied to equal the current market price of a share. Based on last year's earnings per share, this is called the historic P/E ratio, and on forecast earnings, the prospective P/E ratio.

4. EARNINGS PER SHARE - The after-tax profits of a company attributable to ordinary shareholders, calculated on a per share basis (by dividing the number of shares in issue into the after-tax profits).

5. NET ASSET VALUE - The total assets of a company, less all of its short and long-term liabilities, provisions and charges. Sometimes simply abbreviated to NAV.

6. NET ASSET VALUE PER SHARE - The net asset value of a company divided by the number of ordinary shares in issue. The NAV per share is a particularly pertinent measure of value with property companies and investment trusts, which are asset based.

GENERAL MARKET DEFINITIONS

- BEAR - an investor who is pessimistic about the market outlook and believes that share prices will fall.

- BULL - an investor who is optimistic about the market outlook and believes that share prices will rise.

- STAG - an applicant for shares in a new issue who, if successful, intends to sell for a quick profit.

- CALL - an option to buy a share or a commodity.

- PUT - an option to sell a share or a commodity.

- BLUE CHIPS - top companies which are well established and held in high esteem by the investment community.

- F.T. INDICES - there are two main indices in common usage in the UK — the FT-SE 100 Index of 100 leading stocks and the FT-A All-Share Index of about 700 top companies. The more widely- based index, the FT-A All-Share, gives the best guide to what is happening in the market as a whole, but the FT-SE 100 Index (Footsie) is more often referred to by the media.

- OFFER FOR SALE - a method of arranging a new issue on the stock market, inviting the general public to apply for shares.

- PLACING - a method of arranging for a company to be quoted on the stockmarket through a placing of shares by a stockbroker or merchant bank with a number of institutional and private clients.

- SHELL - a small, nondescript company, which usually has negligible assets, but has the advantage of a Stock Exchange quotation. Entrepreneurs frequently inject businesses into shells to obtain a back-door quotation, in most cases because their companies have too short a record, or some other deficiency, which would preclude using a more conventional route.

- CHARTISTS - technical analysts, as chartists are sometimes called, believe that a chart showing the history of a share price reflects the hopes and fears of all investors and is essentially based upon the only indisputable fact — how the share price has performed in the market-place. Chartists believe that 'the trend is your friend' and that they can predict future movements from the past pattern of the chart. The opposite of a technical analyst is a 'fundamentalist', who believes that the underlying net worth of a company and the record and trend of earnings are more important in determining the future of the share price.

- INTERIM - the formal statement to the Stock Exchange and shareholders of the trading results for the first half of a company's financial year. In most cases, companies also pay interim dividends to shareholders.

- OPTION - the right (with no obligation) to buy or sell a share or other security. Usually, options are granted to directors of a company and key management to provide them with an extra incentive.

- WARRANT - an option to buy a company's shares (usually over a long period).

INDEX

Page numbers in italic refer to tables and charts

PHOTOGRAPH CREDITS

CAMERA PRESS. FT PHOTOGRAPH. PICTOR INTERNATIONAL. TONY STONE WORLDWIDE. MONOPOLY is a registered trademark of Parker Brothers, a division of Tonka Corporation, Beverly 01915, USA. Used under license by Waddington Games Ltd. © All rights reserved. Our thanks to the following companies for supplying photographs: Airtours, Amersham International, BDM, Betterware, The Body Shop, Cadbury Schweppes, Clarke Foods, Domestic & General, English China Clays, Farepak, Glass's Guide, Kalon Group, Hanson, Iceland Frozen Foods, ICS Group, Medeva, MTL Instruments, Next, Photo-Me International, Rentokil, Rosehaugh, SmithKline Beecham, Speyhawk, Tomkins, Virgin Group, Wassall, Williams Holdings and Weir Group. Also thanks to Joseph Granville.